FORD AOD Transmissions

Rebuilding and Modifying the AOD, AODE and 4R70W

George Reid

CarTech®

CarTech®

CarTech®, Inc.
6118 Main Street
North Branch, MN 55056
Phone: 651-277-1200 or 800-551-4754
Fax: 651-277-1203
www.cartechbooks.com

Edit by Bob Wilson
Layout by Monica Seiberlich

ISBN 978-1-61325-114-0
Item No. SA279

Library of Congress Cataloging-in-Publication Data

Reid, George.
Ford AOD transmissions / by George Reid.
pages cm
ISBN 978-1-61325-114-0
1. Ford automobile–Transmission devices, Automatic–Maintenance and repair. I. Title.

TL263.R45 2014
629.2›4460288--dc23

2013043956

Written, edited, and designed in the U.S.A.
Printed in China
10 9 8 7

Title Page: *Transmission-assembly fixtures take on many different uses. Optimum for your build is a transmission-holding fixture, and they aren't all that expensive. Transmission tailshaft housings used as holding fixtures also work well.*

Back Cover Photos

Top Left: *You want precision measuring tools such as calipers and micrometers to measure clutch steels, bore diameter, and a host of other dimensions. Because automatic transmissions are all about math and precision assembly, you must understand practical application if you're going to do it yourself.*

Top Right: *Although transmission shops often have clutch spring compressors for piston and clutch removal, you can do this at home with C-clamps. Be sure to always use eye and face protection.*

Middle Left: *As you install the new intermediate clutch piston seals, keep in mind the seal lips must point toward the pressure source or inside the pump housing bore. Pressure against the seal lip is self-sealing and fail-safe. If you point the seal lip toward the intermediate clutches, you will have an internal hydraulic leak and no intermediate clutch function.*

Middle Right: *This is the TransGo SK AODE Shift Kit for all 1991–2007 AODEs, 4R70Ws, and 4R75Ws. The SK AODE kit eliminates slippage and damaging harsh shifts. It improves both shift firmness and timing. The SK AODE kit changes the 4-2 downshift to a 4-3-2 downshift, which prevents roller clutch failure. It also improves overdrive band and forward clutch engagement via increased line pressure.*

Bottom Left: *Incorrectly installing the AOD/AODE/4R70W torque converter is an easy mistake to make. Get it wrong and you trash the transmission's front pump. Rock the converter back and forth. You should be able to feel it seat three times with an AOD and twice with an AODE/4R70W.*

Bottom Right: *Use proper installation equipment such as a transmission jack or a floor jack with a transmission cradle. Make sure the torque converter is properly seated. It is easy for the converter to slip off input shafts and pump drives and wind up with a faulty installation and pump failure. If you can fit your hand between the converter and the bellhousing, it is not properly seated.*

DISTRIBUTION BY:

Europe
PGUK
63 Hatton Garden
London EC1N 8LE, England
Phone: 020 7061 1980 • Fax: 020 7242 3725
www.pguk.co.uk

Australia
Renniks Publications Ltd.
3/37-39 Green Street
Banksmeadow, NSW 2109, Australia
Phone: 2 9695 7055 • Fax: 2 9695 7355
www.renniks.com

Canada
Login Canada
300 Saulteaux Crescent
Winnipeg, MB, R3J-3T2 Canada
Phone: 800 665 1148 • Fax: 800 665 0103
www.lb.ca

CONTENTS

Acknowledgments

A book of this magnitude could not have been accomplished without help from savvy transmission-building professionals and companies that provided tremendous support, including friends and professionals who have helped me time after time and were willing, once again, to put aside their own work to help me.

When Ron Hazleton of Transmission Rebuilding Company (TRC) in Chatsworth, California, was contacted about this book project, he jumped at the opportunity not so much for the notoriety and exposure, but for the opportunity to teach readers about automatic transmission function, rebuilding, and service. Ron is a born educator and a seasoned transmission builder. His team of in-house professionals has the same committed attitude about this subject. Ron took valuable time from his job to walk me through a detailed AODE/4R70W rebuild, employing methodical detail throughout. He gave me a close-up look at the most advanced version of the automatic overdrive, which instills confidence in one of the best Ford automatics ever built.

Up the road in Canyon Country, California, are Brian Fortune and his father, Tom, of Tom's Transmissions along Sierra Highway, who built an AOD for this book. Brian is a very patient man who went over the top for this book as well as for my previous C4/C6 book. Brian walked me through every phase of an AOD, showing me how to incorporate AODE/4R70W advanced improvements into Ford's original automatic overdrive.

Through the years Mike Stewart of Mike's Transmission in Lancaster, California, has always been involved in my projects. Mike hasn't been just a cohort in crime for editorial efforts; he's a great friend as well. Were it not for Mike, I wouldn't know a forward clutch from a rear planet carrier.

Great books don't happen without the tireless efforts of other professional shops, too: Leon's Transmissions in Reseda and AAMCO Transmissions in North Hollywood, both located in suburban Los Angeles, just to name two others. Gentlemen, I thank you for your unyielding assistance with this book and a host of others. I will never be able to thank you enough.

George Reid

What is a Workbench® Book?

This Workbench® Series book is the only book of its kind on the market. No other book offers the same combination of detailed hands-on information and revealing color photographs to illustrate transmission rebuilding and modifying. Rest assured, you have purchased an indispensable companion that will expertly guide you, one step at a time, through each important stage of the rebuilding process. This book is packed with real-world techniques and practical tips for expertly performing rebuild procedures, not vague instructions or unnecessary processes. At-home mechanics or enthusiast builders strive for professional results, and the instruction in our Workbench® Series books help you realize pro-caliber results. Hundreds of photos guide you through the entire process from start to finish, with informative captions containing comprehensive instructions for every step of the process.

The step-by-step photo procedures also contain many additional photos that show how to install high-performance components, modify stock components for special applications, or even call attention to assembly steps that are critical to proper operation or safety. These are labeled with unique icons. These symbols represent an idea, and photos marked with the icons contain important, specialized information.

Here are some of the icons found in Workbench® books:

Important!
Calls special attention to a step or procedure, so that the procedure is correctly performed. This prevents damage to a vehicle, system, or component.

Save Money
Illustrates a method or alternate method of performing a rebuild step that will save money but still give acceptable results.

Torque Fasteners
Illustrates a fastener that must be properly tightened with a torque wrench at this point in the rebuild. The torque specs are usually provided in the step.

Special Tool
Illustrates the use of a special tool that may be required or can make the job easier (caption with photo explains further).

Performance Tip
Indicates a procedure or modification that can improve performance. The step most often applies to high-performance or racing engines.

Critical Inspection
Indicates that a component must be inspected to ensure proper operation of the engine.

Precision Measurement
Illustrates a precision measurement or adjustment that is required at this point in the rebuild.

Professional Mechanic Tip
Illustrates a step in the rebuild that non-professionals may not know. It may illustrate a shortcut or a trick to improve reliability, prevent component damage, etc.

Documentation Required
Illustrates a point in the rebuild where the reader should write down a particular measurement, size, part number, etc. for later reference or photograph a part, area, or system of the vehicle for future reference.

Tech Tip
Tech Tips provide brief coverage of important subject matter that doesn't naturally fall into the text or step-by-step procedures of a chapter. Tech Tips contain valuable hints, important info, or outstanding products that professionals have discovered after years of work. These will add to your understanding of the process, and help you get the most power, economy, and reliability from your engine.

CHAPTER 1

HISTORY AND EVOLUTION

The prosperous postwar years provided time to forget about the Great Depression and fuel/material shortages. We became wasteful in the years following World War II because fuel was in plentiful supply. Gas wars were common, with fuel at giveaway prices. Overdrive, which had been quite common prior to World War II, faded away amid cheap and plentiful gasoline and low-buck engine overhauls.

When the Arab Oil Embargo unfolded during the winter of 1973–1974, it was a rude awakening for spoiled American motorists. Large-displacement carbureted V-8s, heavy automobiles, and 2- and 3-speed straight-drive automatics came with a price at the pump. Fuel had long been cheap and plentiful, and it was a great ride while it lasted. However, what seemed short-lived would be our ultimate destiny: higher fuel prices. When the second oil crisis arrived in 1979, it brought with it increased fuel-economy standards imposed by the federal government. This time Detroit was ready with more-fuel-efficient automatics with direct mechanical lockup torque converters. And Ford was no exception.

Ford's Automatic Overdrive (AOD) entered service in 1980 in full-size Fords, Mercurys, and Lincolns. What makes the AOD rugged is its geartrain, consisting of a Ravigneaux compound planetary gearset borrowed from the older, time-proven MX, FX, and FMX transmission family. Ford fitted these internals to a fresh cast-aluminum case with an overdrive unit.

Ford's fuel-efficiency approach began first with locking torque converter 3-speed automatic transmissions such as the Ford C5, which was an updated version of the venerable C4. Chrysler did the same thing with its 904 Torqueflite with a locking converter and its "Lean Burn" electronic engine/powertrain control system in the late 1970s. General Motors joined the crowd with its Turbo 200 and 200-4R.

The AOD

Ford's automatic overdrive (AOD), first introduced in 1980, was the first domestic automatic overdrive transmission. General Motors and Chrysler swiftly followed. Chrysler added overdrive units to existing 3-speed automatics: the 904 and 727. General Motors further developed the 200 into a 200-4R with overdrive, and from there the all-new 700-R4 purpose-built automatic overdrive.

Although the automatic overdrive might seem intimidating when compared with older C4, C6, and FMX 3-speed automatics, there's really nothing to it aside from add-on hydromechanicals and direct overdrive lockup to eliminate wasteful slippage.

Ford's all-new AOD in full-size Fords, Mercurys, and Lincolns was a fresh design, yet it incorporated existing tried-and-proven Ravigneaux geartrain components borrowed from the BorgWarner FMX parts bin. The AOD is rugged and dependable thanks to the use of these time-proven components. It took quite a few years for Ford to get the AOD dialed in to be a solid performer, however, and this occurred with help from the aftermarket and off-road racers. The AOD had durability problems, most notably in the overdrive unit, which was a new design using unproven components. Ultimately, the 1993 Lincoln Mark VIII AOD Electronic Control (AODE)/4R70W's wider overdrive drum and band solved the problem.

More than 30 years into its service life, the AOD has proven to be an outstanding transmission for street and strip use thanks to effective engineering refinements. Vintage Ford enthusiasts love the AOD for its simplicity, durability, and an array of installation kits available in the aftermarket. California Pony Cars, in particular, offers everything you need to swap the AOD into a classic Mustang. There's also Performance Automotive Transmission Center (PATC), which offers a variety of AOD and 5R55 swap kits and parts. Speedway Motors has swap kits for the Ford flathead V-8. Bronco Graveyard is yet another source. There are

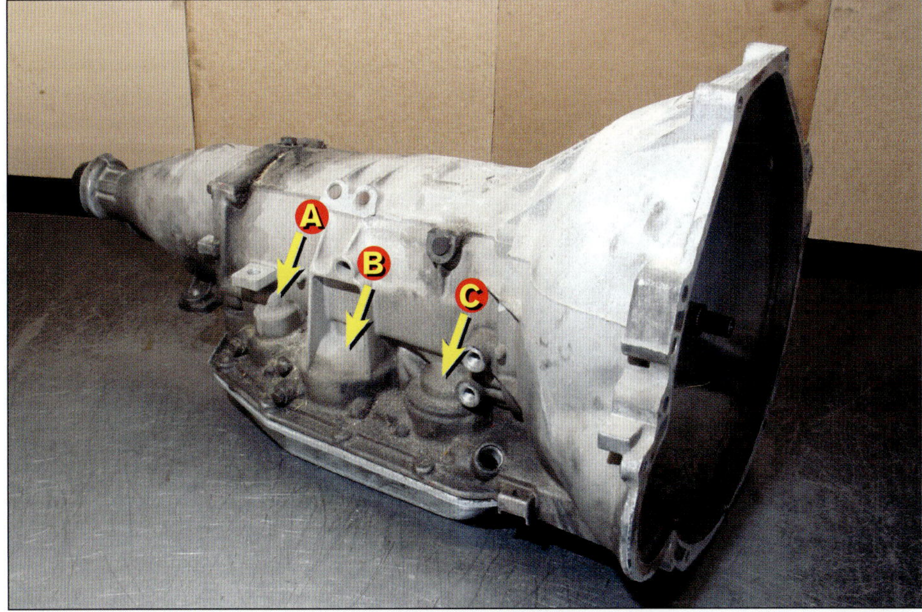

This is the AOD passenger's side with dipstick tube access, cooler line connections, and pressure ports. As you can see from the case design, the AOD has two servos and bands with an accumulator at the rear. From left to right in the case are the shift accumulator (A), low-reverse band servo (B), and overdrive band servo (C). All are accessed by pulling the pan and valve body. Because the AOD has an integral bellhousing, it is limited in application. Adaptor kits are available for the AOD for the FE-series big-block, the Y-Block, Bronco, older F-Series, and more.

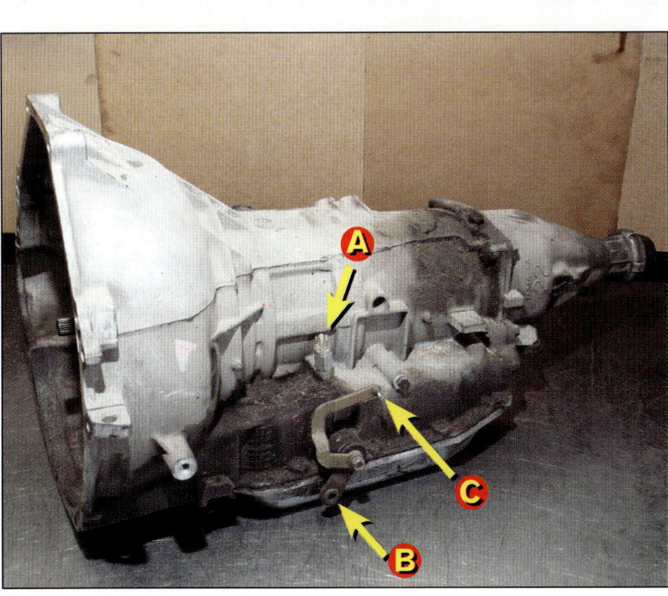

The driver's side of the AOD shows the linear multi-pin connector backup light and neutral safety switch (A), the manual shift lever pointed downward at 7 o'clock (B), and the dogleg TV cable connection (C). The bellhousing threaded boss is for the TV cable linkage from the engine.

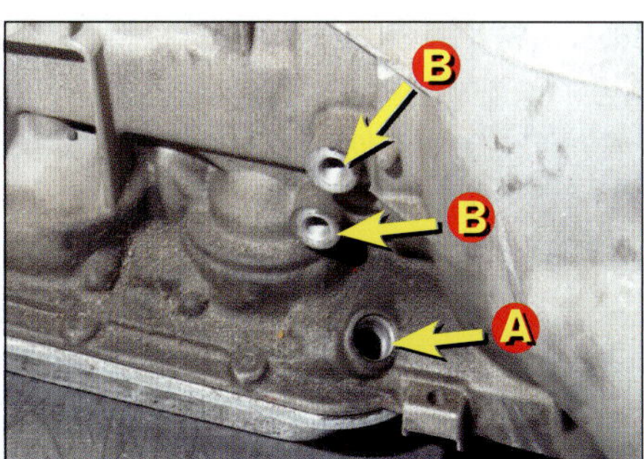

Here are the dipstick tube (A) and cooler line (B) ports. The AOD dipstick tube clears most firewalls on classic vehicles such as the Mustang, Cougar, Fairlane, Torino, F-Series trucks, and Broncos. Aftermarket dipstick tubes fit those vehicles if stock tubes won't.

The AOD's torque converter and bellhousing are designed for a 164-tooth flexplate, a small-block V-8, and large 6-cylinder blocks. AOD torque converter installation is tricky. You must confirm that it is fully seated on the two input shafts and the front pump drive. If it isn't fully seated, you can expect extensive damage and transmission failure.

The AOD has two input shafts: a large hollow main input shaft and a smaller solid overdrive/torque converter lockup shaft, which is more for light-duty cruising once you get up to speed. The largest outer shaft is the torque converter's stator support and it does not rotate.

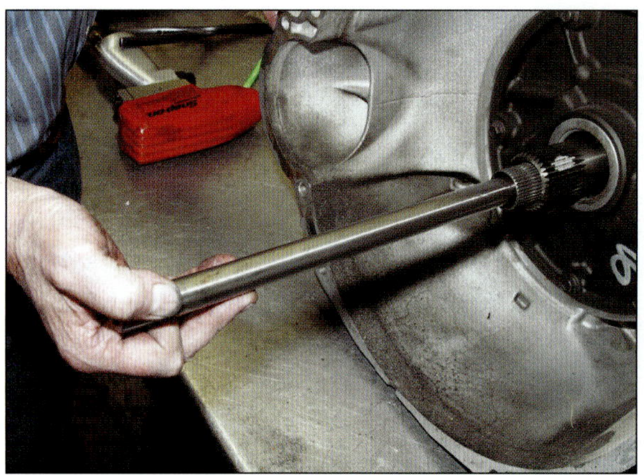

This is the smaller solid overdrive/locking converter input shaft, which transfers power to the overdrive unit in lockup only. What makes torque converter installation so important is getting the torque converter fully seated on the stator, main input shaft, and this smaller lockup shaft. The converter must also fully seat into the front pump drive rotor. It is all performed by feel.

The AOD's Ravigneaux compound planetary gearset is the old-school, tried-and-proven durable geartrain borrowed from BorgWarner's cast-iron FMX transmission. The Ravigneaux gearset is the workhorse that does the work of two planetaries.

This is the AOD's stamped-steel pan with the words "Automatic Overdrive" and "Metric" for quick identification. The AOD pan is shaped differently from the AODE/4R70W pan and does not interchange.

several sources that enable you to put the AOD behind an FE big-block.

The AOD is a true hydromechanical 4-speed automatic transmission controlled by a manual shifter and throttle valve (TV) cable. The TV cable, tied to the vehicle's throttle linkage, works like a kickdown linkage, yet it is more finite in its execution because it does the work of both a kickdown (downshift) linkage and vacuum modulator used on earlier Ford automatics. There is no vacuum modulator or kickdown linkage with the AOD as we see with the older C3, C4, C6, and FMX transmissions; only the lone TV cable.

The C3, C4, C6, and FMX transmissions have vacuum modulators to control shift-points, depending

With a Ravigneaux compound planetary gearset, load is distributed across a broad surface area for smoothness and less wear. It also has the benefits of two gearsets in one, which offers some weight reduction and engineering simplicity (with fewer parts).

Here's the AOD's Ravigneaux gearset as viewed from inside where planet gears wrap around the sun gear (not shown) and shell. This stamped assembly, known as the center support, supports the geartrain.

The AOD's internals: main input shaft, reverse clutch drum (overdrive band), forward clutch, and direct clutch cylinder. This is how they go together and fit into the transmission case.

The AOD's forward clutch assembly is driven by the main input shaft. On the bench is the direct clutch, which delivers power to the output shaft.

The AOD's cast-iron and steel gear pump provides hydraulic control pressure and lubrication. Included with the front pump is the intermediate clutch piston, which holds the forwardmost clutch pack in the case immediately behind the pump.

The AOD's front pump case casting number tells you which front pump you have. Although there were virtually no engineering changes to this pump during its production life, there are variations in this casting number, depending upon when it was cast.

upon throttle position and manifold vacuum. They also have a throttle-controlled kickdown linkage, which works with the vacuum modulator to control shift-points mostly for wide-open throttle (WOT) downshift. The vacuum modulator finitely controls line pressure. The kickdown delivers maximum line pressure at WOT. The AOD eliminates the vacuum modulator by relying strictly on throttle position via the TV cable to control shift-points. Proper adjustment of the TV cable is crucial. Improper adjustment can lead to transmission failure, which means it must be performed strictly by the book to prevent slippage and clutch/band failure.

The AOD is equipped with two friction bands and clutch drums: one low-reverse band and clutch drum and one band and clutch pack for overdrive. There are also two one-way clutches, and four friction clutches. The geartrain consists of a Ravigneaux compound planetary gear package also used in the FMX, MX, and FX transmissions employing two sun gears and a dual pinion set that provides four forward gears and one reverse. This makes the AOD a tough competitor in the

Here, you can see the difference between a standard AOD reverse drum (right) and the 1993-up Lincoln AODE/4R70W reverse/overdrive drum (left). The wider Lincoln reverse drum and overdrive band hold better due to increased surface/friction area. The wider reverse drum/overdrive band is what you want for any AOD build because of its greater holding power and reduced chance of failure. Never use the wider band without using the wider drum.

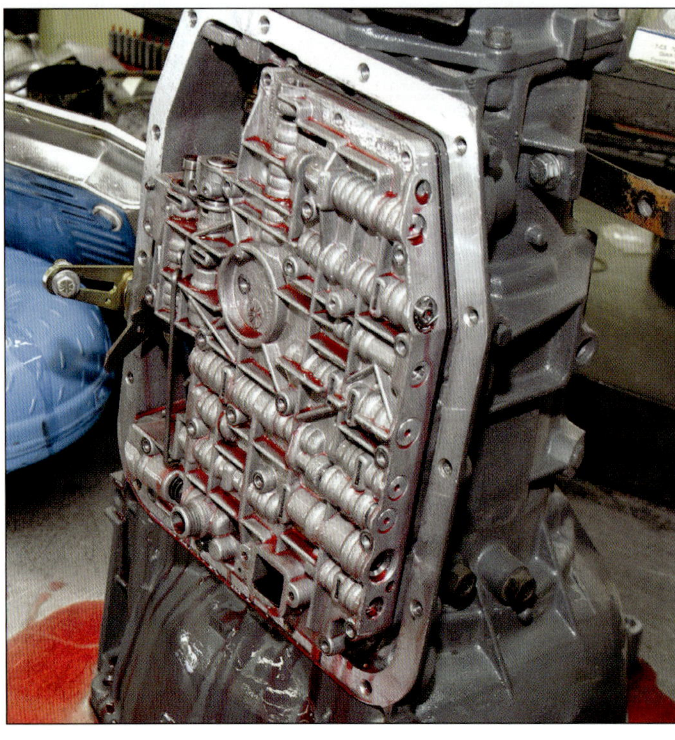

The AOD's valve body didn't change much throughout its production life. What makes it different from the AODE/4R70W valve body is its throttle valve function rather than computer control.

Look for the Ford casting number on main cases and valve bodies for an indication of when the part was produced. This is a 1980 AOD RF-E0AP-7A092-AF valve body.

Here's an RF-E9DP-7006-AA AOD main case, an engineering revision time frame of 1989. "RF" is believed to mean Rouge Foundry (Dearborn, Michigan).

This is the multi-pin backup light/neutral safety switch for AOD only. It is a linear switch operated by a cam on the manual shift linkage inside the case. It prohibits starting in any drive gear range and illuminates the backup lights while in reverse.

The AOD is an old-school automatic with hydromechanical function and a conventional tailshaft flyweight valve governor that affects upshifts and downshifts based on vehicle speed. It has a direct effect on control pressure and shift-points. This governor is calibrated to vehicle weight and size, which means there are variations that you need to be aware of, especially if you've purchased an AOD core of unknown origin.

This AOD tailshaft housing with RF-E0AP-7A040-BD indicates a 1980 original casting from Rouge Foundry. The "E0AP" part of the casting number doesn't always mean it was cast in 1980; it means there were no engineering changes since 1980. The number "25" here is the cavity number, which indicates which sand-cast mold the piece was cast from. In other words, a bunch of identical sand-casting "cavities" were used on cast-iron or aluminum parts in mass production. Cavity numbers help the foundry find any casting issues. On main AOD cases, you find the cavity number on the bellhousing.

On the backup light/neutral safety switch, the copper pin rides a manual shift linkage cam that moves the pin in linear fashion to open the start circuit or fire the backup lights. This switch is available from Late Model Restorations (PN SW2276). The harness and multi-pin plug is available from Ron Francis Wiring (PN PG-057).

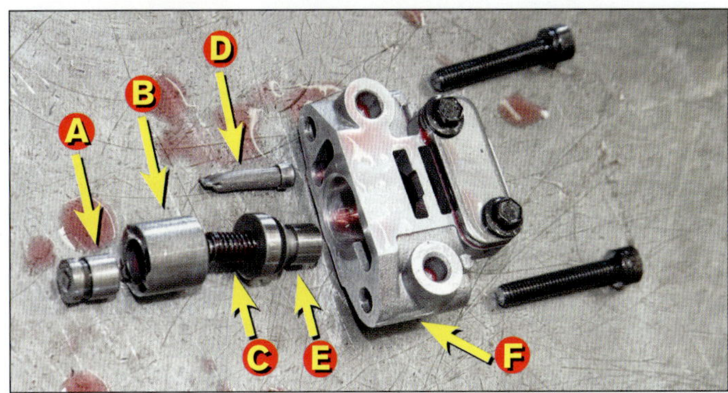

This disassembled AOD governor demonstrates function. From left is the (A) plug, (B) sleeve, (C) spring and retainer clip, (D) valve piston, (E) screen, and (F) main governor body with cover plate. The counterweight is not shown, but it houses the valve assembly and counterweights the complete assembly. The governor valve piston is spring loaded and operates against both spring load and centrifugal force. As the output shaft spins faster with vehicle speed, the valve piston overcomes spring pressure and line pressure goes to work. This affects shift-points as well as throttle valve movement. It also affects both upshift and downshift points. Use a stiffer spring and you get a higher shift-point. Calibration is based on spring pressure.

complicated world of automatic overdrive transmissions.

Because most AOD transmissions have the six-bolt bellhousing design first introduced for 1965, they fit behind any small-block V-8 or large 240- or 300-ci 6-cylinder engine. Smaller five-bolt bellhousing V-8s prior to 1965 do not bolt to the AOD. However, there are aftermarket adaptor kits that allow you to bolt the AOD, AODE, and 4R70W to big-block Ford V-8s. This means the AOD has become one of the most trusted automatics in history.

The AOD has a filter retained with three fine-thread bolts and a 10-mm socket. The filter should never be cleaned and returned to service. Always replace it during a fluid change.

This is the AOD manual shift mechanism (left) and throttle valve linkage (right) with the valve body removed. The manual valve detent is a hollow shaft with the throttle valve shaft inside. Both have seals that should be replaced during a rebuild. This application has a Lokar aftermarket external linkage for column shift.

With the AOD valve body removed, two servo pistons and an accumulator are visible. From left to right are the overdrive band servo, low-reverse servo, and the 3-4 shift accumulator. The 3-4 shift accumulator was dropped in 1989 with the addition of a revised valve body and plate. If you use a 1980–1988 AOD valve body, you must have the 3-4 shift accumulator.

Here is the AOD main case with the servo/accumulator covers and pistons removed. Ultimately, Ford eliminated the accumulator in production, which is why some AOD cores are not so equipped. The 3-4 shift accumulator was phased out in the 1989 model year due to leak issues. The valve body is also different to accommodate this production change; it employs a revised separator plate. If your AOD doesn't have a 3-4 shift accumulator, don't worry about installing one.

The easiest way to identify the AOD is the "Automatic Overdrive Metric" wording along with the Ford Blue Oval stamped into its 14-bolt galvanized steel pan. The AOD, like the C6, is a one-piece casting that includes bellhousing and main case, which makes the AOD different from the C3, C4, and FMX transmissions with separate bolt-on bellhousings. Instead of a conventional rotary backup light/neutral safety switch at the manual shift linkage as seen with older Ford automatics, the AOD has a screw-in multi-pin linear connector backup light/neutral safety switch on the left-hand side above the manual shift and TV cable linkage.

The real beauty of the AOD transmission is its easy fitment into just about any Ford application. Thanks to the perseverance of the aftermarket, such as California Pony Cars, it has become easy to swap the AOD into a vintage Ford, Mercury, or Lincoln with a variety of installation kits, which makes the AOD an

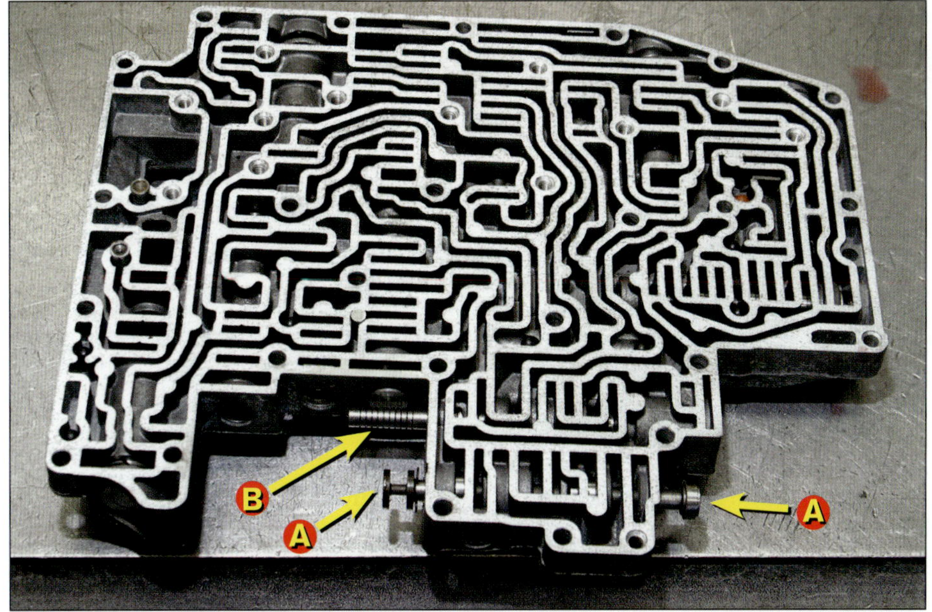

The AOD valve body mates with the main transmission case and is fitted with a manual shift valve (A) and a shift modulation throttle valve (B). The manual shift valve has been offered two basic ways: with an internal detent and with an external bolt-on roller detent. The throttle valve, which varies control pressure based on throttle position, depends on TV cable adjustment. With optimum cable tension, upshifts occur exactly when they're supposed to, in synch with throttle position. Not enough tension and upshifts come too early. Too much tension and upshifts come late.

This AOD with a column shift shows the Lokar manual shift bell crank and TV cable installed in a vintage F-Series truck with FE big-block power. If you have a column shift, the manual shifter at the transmission points downward at 6 o'clock. Here, the Lokar TV cable (left) is disconnected.

A big improvement in efficiency with the AOD is the use of Torrington (needle) bearings throughout to reduce internal friction. Although there are some thrust washers in the AOD geartrain, friction is greatly reduced.

excellent choice for any classic car project. If you already have an AOD in your late-model Ford, you understand this transmission's benefits in terms of smooth operation and improved fuel efficiency. Key to getting along with the AOD is learning as much as possible about its function and how to properly execute a successful rebuild and tune.

Aside from the benefit of overdrive in the AOD, the other benefit is direct drive from the torque converter shell to the overdrive unit. What makes this different from most automatic overdrives is where lockup takes place: inside the overdrive unit instead of the torque converter via an inner input shaft. This feature offers non-slip direct drive in fourth gear (overdrive) and to some degree in third gear as well.

Do a gentle throttle tip-in and get both slippage and torque multiplication in third and fourth gears. Relax the throttle to get overdrive lockup and fuel-efficient direct drive between torque converter shell and output shaft. This is known as "split-torque." It occurs when the transmission comes out of overdrive lockup during throttle tip-in for mild acceleration where you are on the torque converter getting torque multiplication. With torque multiplication, you get 2 to 2½ times your engine's torque.

The split-torque feature enables greater efficiency with torque multiplication as needed with throttle tip-in and straight drive with no slippage at cruise. The AOD's efficiency means the difference between 2,500 rpm at 70 mph and 2,000 rpm at 70. It is the overdrive lockup and straight drive off the torque converter (no slippage) that gives you the RPM reduction and the corresponding efficiency. It also makes the difference between 15 and 20 mpg. In addition, there is the benefit of less wear and tear with lower cruise RPM.

AOD/AODE Gear Ratios

First Gear	2.40:1
Second Gear	1.46:1
Third Gear	1.00:1
Overdrive	0.66:1
Reverse	2.00:1

Torque Converter Installation

Torque converter installation is very tricky with the AOD. It is strictly a matter of feel and getting the converter to slip onto the stator and primary and secondary input shafts. Get this wrong and expect immediate transmission failure on start-up. Work the converter back and forth with gentle pressure. You should experience a triple seating onto the stator and outer and inner shafts. The converter should turn freely. If you can fit your hand between the converter shell and bellhousing, the torque converter is not properly seated. ■

AODE/4R70W

To improve durability and make engine and transmission function more cohesive, Ford introduced the AODE in 1991. AODE, or AOD Electronic Control, delivers precision operation thanks to more unified engine and transmission electronic control. No TV cable adjustment, just predictable computer-controlled operation based on factory calibration, vehicle speed, and throttle position. The AODE was originally conceived for a new generation of overhead-cam Modular V-8s that first arrived in the 1991 Lincoln Town Car. The AODE was also installed behind the 5.0L and 5.8L Ford pushrod V-8s beginning in 1991. The AODE's gearing gave these pushrod small-blocks extra snap under acceleration.

Although the AODE is similar to the AOD, there are important differences to be aware of before attempting a rebuild. The AODE really is a different transmission entirely even though it shares similar architecture. It has a different main case, valve body, torque converter, front pump assembly, input shaft, and other vital components. To improve shift quality, Ford eliminated the

The AODE (electronically controlled AOD) arrived in 1991 to merge engine and transmission function for better performance and fuel economy. The AODE and 4R70W transmissions were an all-new AOD case designed for electronic interaction with engine controls.

The AODE and 4R70W are essentially the same AOD-based transmission. This is a 1997 4R70W with a speedometer drive and output shaft speed sensor. Visible here is the manual shift lever for a column shift. Missing is the backup light/neutral safety switch at the manual shift shaft.

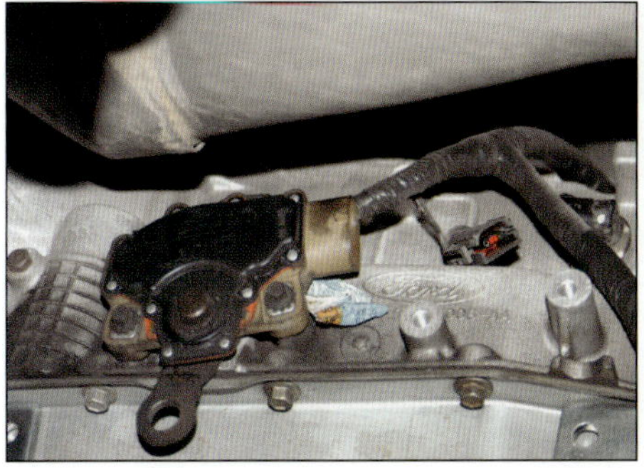

This is the backup light/neutral safety switch on a 4R70W transmission. Just above this switch is the output shaft speed sensor. It works hand in hand with the PCM to unify engine and transmission cohesiveness.

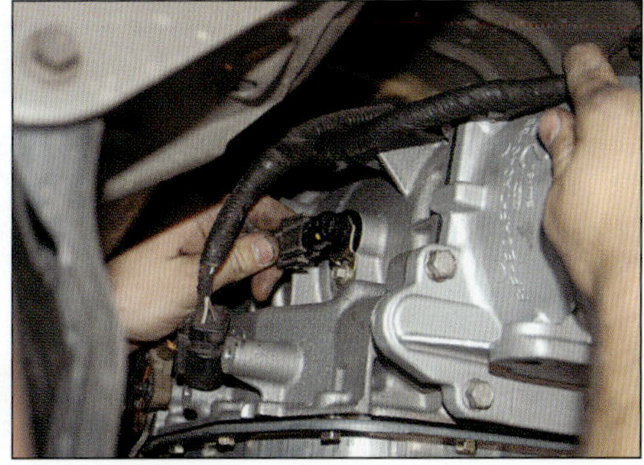

The output-shaft speed sensor and plug are located on the driver's side of an AODE/4R70W. The multiplex plug to the left is for the backup light/ neutral safety switch on the driver's side of the transmission.

On the AODE/4R70W's passenger's side is the shift solenoid and converter lockup multiplex plug that ties the transmission to the PCM. This connection eliminates the need for a TV cable and mechanical shift modulation.

This is the electronic speedometer drive sensor that takes the place of a cable drive and (phased-out) mechanical speedometer. However, the AODE/4R70W output shaft housing still accommodates a mechanical speedometer drive.

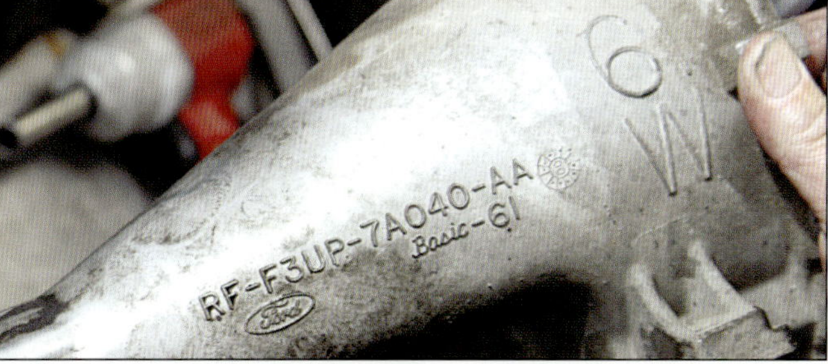

This is the tailshaft housing for an AODE or 4R70W with casting number RF-F3UP-7A040-AA and cavity number 61. This particular cast-aluminum tailshaft housing was produced by The Basic Aluminum Casting Company in Cleveland, Ohio, for the Ford Motor Company. The sand casting it came from was cavity 61, meaning there were at least 61 molds.

The AODE and 4R70W have a larger input shaft that connects a locking torque converter to the overdrive unit. The AODE/4R70W is different because there is one input shaft instead of both a primary and intermediate shaft.

The AODE/4R70W manual shift mechanism is basically the same as the AOD except it has no linear backup light/neutral safety switch. Instead, this function is outside the case. This is the pressure control solenoid, which is a large, heavy electromagnet that pulses to control system pressure. If it malfunctions, you may experience severe transmission damage.

The AODE/4R70W valve body is different from, and not interchangeable with, the AOD. It lacks the throttle valve of the AOD. The system pressure programming and shift-points are computer controlled instead of being mechanically modulated. The manual shifter valve has a bolt-on detent to lock shift positions.

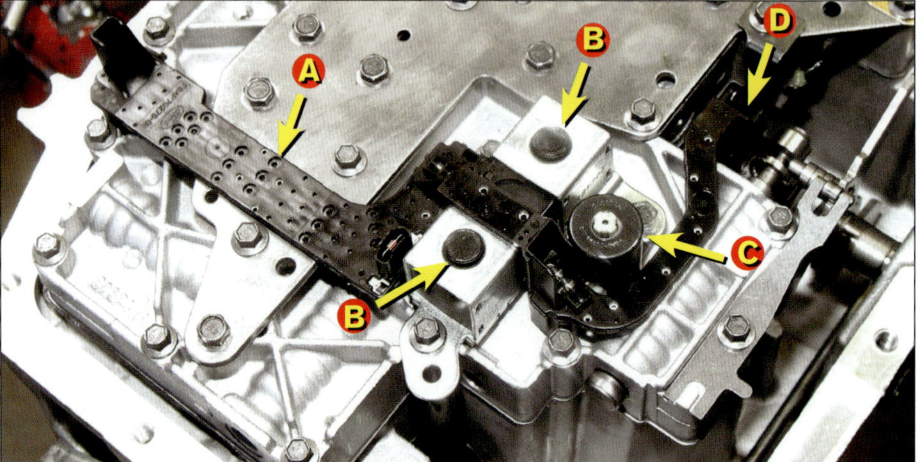

The AODE originally had a raw wiring harness that connected the multiplex system plug to the shift control solenoids and converter lockup solenoid. The 4R70W has a clever wire channel (A) that anchors into place with good security. The two side-by-side solenoids (B) are shift-control solenoids. The one lone solenoid (C) is for converter lockup in overdrive. At the far right near the shifter is the pressure control solenoid connection (D).

The AODE and 4R70W have a press-in filter requiring no tools for removal and installation. Take extra care to ensure the rubber seal and filter are secure before buttoning up. Remember, never reuse a filter.

Ford casting numbers can be found on all AODE, 4R70W, and 4R75 castings. These numbers are key to knowing which transmission you have and what parts should be used.

The AODE/4R70W transmission pan is unique to these electronically controlled units because it employs a different bolt pattern and a deeper sump for improved cooling and lubrication.

This is the AODE/4R70W planetary gearset, which uses an improved first-gear ratio for better acceleration. The AODE/4R70W gearset swaps into an AOD to get that better 2.84:1 to 1.55:1 1-2 upshift and holeshot.

The AODE/4R70W front pump is a totally new gerotor aluminum design that delivers the same pressures as the AOD iron gear pump, but at a greater volume at low engine speeds.

The AODE/4R70W multiplex plug connection enables the electronically controlled AOD to work seamlessly with engine operation. Instead of a TV cable that can move out of adjustment, it uses electronics for precision function.

The updated 4R75W and 4R75E have two shaft sensors for input and output shafts for greater cohesiveness between the engine and transmission. The 4R75-series transmission has a different main case to accommodate both sensors.

4R70W Gear Ratios

First	2.84:1
Second	1.55:1
Third	1.00:1
Overdrive	0.70:1
Reverse	2.23:1

split-torque function in third and fourth gears.

Like the AOD (and FMX), the AODE has a Ravigneaux compound planetary gearset employing two sun gears and a dual pinion set offering four forward gears and one reverse. Also like the AOD, there are two bands, two one-way clutches, and four friction clutches to get the job done.

The AODE name was used from 1991 to 1992. The 4R70W (basically an AODE) was introduced in 1993 behind the 4.6L dual overhead cam (DOHC) V-8 only in the new Lincoln Mark VIII. It also appeared in some F-Series trucks that same year.

Another important change from the AOD is the use of a locking torque converter on the AODE and 4R70W instead of the split-torque overdrive unit lockup feature. Ford's explanation for moving away from split torque was to create a more cohesive engine and driveline package. With the AODE/4R70W, throttle tip-in while you're in overdrive disengages the converter clutch, which enables torque multiplication with improved acceleration without having to switch from one input shaft to another. With the AODE and 4R70W it all happens via one input shaft. With the AODE and 4R70W, you have converter clutch engagement and disengagement instead of overdrive lockup.

The AODE front pump, made of aluminum with a steel rotor, is also improved for better flow at idle and increased lubrication and pressure. AOD and AODE front pump rotors differ in the number of rotor teeth and can be identified as such. The AODE/4R70W front pump is about volume and lots of it. The downside to the aluminum pump is somewhat reduced durability.

The AODE/4R70W also uses a new-and-improved valve body with two computer-controlled solenoid packages consisting of two shift solenoids and one converter clutch solenoid. According to Ford, the AODE valve body is thicker for improved strength and durability. Valves in the AODE are made of aluminum instead of steel for decreased weight and improved sealing because both valve body and valves have the same expansion properties.

What makes the 4R70W different from the AODE is lower gear ratios in first and second gears, which improve acceleration. The 4.6L Modular V-8 engine needs this feature more than the 5.0L and 5.8L pushrod V-8s because the 4.6L doesn't have the same torque curve as a small-block. Lowering the AODE's first-gear ratio helped improve standing-start takeoffs with the Modular V-8 engine.

4R75W and 4R75E

The 4R70W has evolved to be an even better transmission with engineering refinements leading to the 4R75W and 4R75E, introduced in 2003, which employ even better computer control thanks to the use of input and output shaft sensors.

Most of the improvements have to do with shift control via the valve body. Torque capacity became better along with gearset durability improvements and a more durable overdrive drum. The 4R75's ring gear has 24 tabs instead of 6 for the output shaft sensor for more precise shift control.

With the 4R75W and 4R75E came an improved front pump and torque converter, as well as the input shaft sensor already mentioned. There's also a refined vehicle speed sensor to fine-tune performance as you drive. Another important development with the 4R75W and 4R75E is additional programming in the powertrain control module (PCM), or computer, that enables use in drive-by-wire vehicles.

TECH TIP

What Does "4R70W" Mean?

4 = 4-Speed
R = Rear Wheel Drive
70 = Input Torque in ft-lbs x 10 = 700 ft-lbs
W = Wide Ratio

Check for External Faults

Because the AODE- and 4R70W-series transmissions are electronically controlled, malfunctions may occur that have nothing to do with the transmission, yet they adversely affect transmission operation.

Check all connections and wiring for breaks and shorts to ground. Check the plugs. All connections must be clean and free of contaminants. All grounds must be solid and free of corrosion. This means every ground in the vehicle. Composite-body vehicles (with body on frame) can be especially troublesome with weak grounds.

If troubleshooting doesn't reveal obvious electrical issues, check the PCM, also known as the electronic control module (ECM). Checking the PCM/ECM requires diagnostic equipment that you are not likely to have in your home garage. If you are expecting a fault code, there would be a Check Engine light to begin with. Most transmission shops have the diagnostic equipment necessary to find a PCM/ECM issue. You can also swap in another PCM/ECM as a test unit.

Ford vehicles with electronically controlled AOD transmissions have a history of PCM-related malfunction that causes the electronic pressure control (EPC) solenoid to fluctuate. At the same time, the engine loses power (random misfire) to protect the transmission. The only solution is to replace or repair the PCM. ■

Ford Part Numbers

Ford part and casting numbers can be confusing, especially if you've never dealt with them before. There are actually two part-numbering systems that apply to the AOD-, AODE-, and 4R70W-series transmissions. The old, more traditional Ford numbering system was used from 1980–1998; then a new system from 1999-up. Both are explained here. The codes listed below are those that apply to the AOD-, AODE-, and 4R70W-series transmissions.

1980–1999

Here is a typical Ford part/casting number:

E9DP–7006–AA
Prefix–Basic Part Number–Suffix

The prefix (first four characters) indicates when the part was originally released for production, what car line it was released for, and what engineering group it came from.

First Position (Decade)

E = 1980–1989 F = 1990–1999

Second Position (Year of Decade)

Indicates the year the part was released by engineering for production.

0 = 1980, 1990	5 = 1985, 1995
1 = 1981, 1991	6 = 1986, 1996
2 = 1982, 1992	7 = 1987, 1997
3 = 1983, 1993	8 = 1988, 1998
4 = 1984, 1994	9 = 1989, 1999

Third Position (Car Line)

A = Ford	T = Light Truck and Bronco
B = Fairmont	Z = Mustang
D = Granada, LTD	4 = Mercury Monarch, Cougar, Marquis
M = Mercury	
S = Thunderbird	7 = Capri

Fourth Position (Engineering Department)

E = Engine
P = Automatic Transmission and Axle
W = Transmission, Axle, and Driveshaft Engineering

However, if you have a service replacement part, the fourth position indicates division, as follows:

Z = Ford Division
Y = Lincoln-Mercury
X = Original Ford Muscle Parts Program
M = Ford Motorsport Special Vehicle Operations or Ford Racing Performance Parts

Basic Part Number

The basic part or casting number is the same whether it is an engineering number or a service number. Automatic transmissions are 6905–6968 and 7000–7999.

Suffix

The suffix tells you the change level. "A" means original status of released part. "B" indicates one engineering change. The entire alphabet is used except for the letters "I" and "L," which could be mistaken for the number "1." If Ford needs to go through the entire alphabet, it starts over again at "AA," "AB," "AC," "AD," and so on.

It is important to understand that part, casting, engineering, and service numbers rarely match one another. The casting number is derived from the actual casting or part, and typically does not match the part, engineering, or service numbers. Unless the casting has been revised, the basic casting number does not change. This means the number you see on the casting does not necessarily match the part number in the Ford Master Parts Catalog. And if the catalog you are using is outdated, as most are, expect even more changes in your Ford dealer's microfiche or computer when it comes to suffixes.

When demand for a part falls below a pre-determined level, Ford discontinues, or N/Rs, the part. N/R means "Not Replaced."

Ford Part Numbers *CONTINUED*

Date Codes

Ford makes it easy to identify transmission castings because there are three foolproof systems in place. First is the casting number, which tells you the engineering level. Second is the casting date code, an alphanumeric code that tells you the exact date the item was cast at the foundry. There is also a foundry logo cast into the piece that tells you where it was cast. And finally, a manufacturing date code is normally stamped into a machined surface, which confirms when the component was manufactured. Casting and manufacture date codes look like this: 4D17. Here's the key:

4 = 1984/1994/2004
D = April
17 = Day

If this code is cast into the piece, it indicates the date the piece was cast at the foundry. If the date code is stamped or inked, it indicates the date of manufacture.

Ford Part Numbers 1999-Up

The new Ford part/casting number system works differently from the old system and takes some getting used to. The only real difference is the first four characters in the part number. The rest of it remains the same.

Instead of seeing part numbers such as C8AE-9510-A, you see something like 3L3P-7006-AA. Here's how it works.

3L3P–7006–AA
Prefix–Basic Part Number–Suffix

First Position (Year)

S = 1995
T = 1996
V = 1997
W = 1998
X = 1999
Y = 2000
1 = 2001
2 = 2002
3 = 2003
4 = 2004
5 = 2005
6 = 2006
7 = 2007
8 = 2008
9 = 2009
A = 2010
B = 2011
C = 2012
D = 2013
E = 2014
F = 2015
G = 2016
H = 2017

Second and Third Positions (Vehicles Equipped with AOD/AODE/4R70W)

C2 = Econoline Van
F3 = Lincoln Continental
F6 = Thunderbird
L1 = Bronco
L3 = F150, F250
R3 = Mustang
R6 = LTD
R9 = Mark VIII
U2 = Motorcraft
W1 = Lincoln Town Car
W2 = Cougar
W3 = Grand Marquis
W4 = DEW98 (1989–1997 Thunderbird and Cougar)
W6 = Thunderbird
W7 = Crown Victoria (1992-up)

Fourth Position (Engineering Responsibility)

E = Engine Engineering, Engine Product
M = Special Vehicle Operations
P = Automatic Transmission and Axle Products
R = Manual Transmission and Axle Products
V = Domestic Special Order Engineering Division
W = Transmission and Axle Product, Manufacturing Engineering (Axle and Driveline)

Basic Part Number

This part number is the same as prior to 1999. It has a cleaner numbering system, however, with left and right specifics. It's also easier to follow and understand because it is more detailed and more specific than the old system.

Suffix

This part number is the same as prior to 1999. Again, it's easier to follow and understand. ■

Getting Started

Before embarking on a Ford automatic overdrive building project, you're going to need a proper work setting and the tools required to do the job. Because automatic transmissions encompass numerous tiny precision parts such as clips, balls, pins, valves, springs, and other items, your shop environment must be neat and orderly, not to mention well lit. Some parts are so small they're easy to overlook, especially with poor lighting and a lot of clutter. With automatic transmissions, there are no unimportant parts. If there are parts left on the workbench when the job is done, you're in trouble.

Cleanliness is never more important than with automatic transmissions. Even the smallest particle of dirt or grit can disturb an automatic transmission's precision tolerances, causing malfunction and poor performance. All it takes is a tiny grain of sand to cause a valve to stick or a seal to tear. Even house dust can be detrimental to transmission function, which is why transmissions should always be bagged whenever they're not being worked on. If you live in a dusty environment, consider taking your bagged transmission inside a clean storage room.

Transmission-assembly fixtures take on many different uses. Optimum for your build is a transmission-holding fixture, and they aren't all that expensive. Transmission tailshaft housings used as holding fixtures also work well.

Safety Precautions

Automatic transmission building creates its share of safety issues.

A clean, organized work setting is what you want for your Ford AOD build. Mike Stewart of Mike's Transmission maintains a clean area for his transmission builds for committed customers from around the world.

Remember, automobiles and components can maim or even kill if you are not careful. Here are a few suggestions to avoid that.

Use Nitrile gloves, which are similar to latex gloves used in hospitals, to protect your hands from harsh chemicals. Solvents can dry out your skin and may also pose a cancer risk.

In addition, you will want to protect your skin from sharp edges. Iron and aluminum castings have their share of sharp edges, as do stamped sheet-metal components. Grind ragged edges smooth to protect yourself from injury and to remove stress risers from castings that can crack.

High-frequency noise from power equipment can damage hearing, so make sure to use earplugs or muffs. Even the background din of shop equipment, electric motors, gear and belt drives, air compressors, and the like will damage hearing over time. Cleaning and drying parts with compressed air, which isn't always recommended, is loud enough to damage hearing.

Eye protection is of utmost importance. If you've ever had metal or other foreign matter removed from your eye, you understand why. Use goggles or safety glasses to protect your eyes from flying debris. Ideally, use wraparound face protection that keeps debris well away from your eyes. And if foreign matter does get in your eyes, go to an emergency room or source of medical care immediately. The longer a piece of metal remains in your eye, the greater the risk of vision loss. Metal corrodes in your eye, causing further damage.

Always use face protection (a full face shield) in addition to eye protection when working around power equipment. A stray bolt launched by a bench grinder can do permanent damage to your eyes or face. Metal particles from a hand-held grinder can cause the same kind of damage. The combination of eye and face protection can prevent the risk of serious injury.

Remember too that how you hold a grinder, cutting wheel, or part determines how safe you are. Always make sure the grinder/cutting wheel rotation is away from you.

Whenever using harsh chemicals such as petroleum or alcohol-based cleaning solvents, protect your lungs with a good respirator. Dust masks are not sufficient protection. A good respirator with charcoal cartridges keeps all chemicals and particulates out of your lungs. The same rule applies to spray paint. Always use a respirator regardless of how well ventilated your shop or driveway is.

Organization

Now that you've got a nice clean place to work, you can get started on your AOD/AODE/4R70W build. The main consideration is order, with a place for everything. Pick up a package of cheap disposable

Organization is important with any automatic transmission build because there are so many details and strict tolerances. What makes this even more critical is the sheer number of parts involved, both large and small.

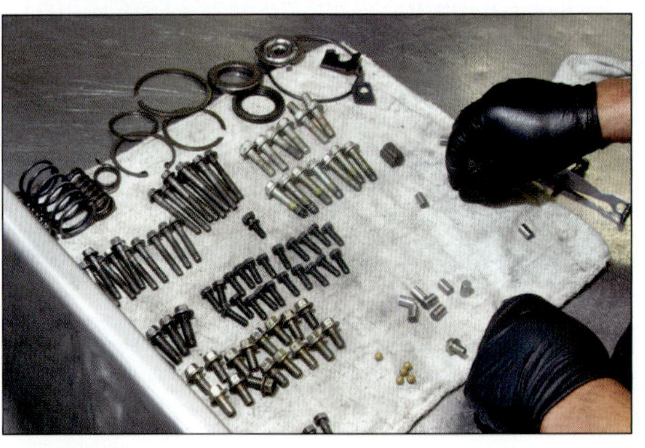

This is organization. Like fasteners are placed alongside one another in compartmentalized fashion. This is how you disassemble, clean, and organize parts for reassembly. Use a tray or baking sheet for parts (avoid cloth if possible).

Transmission shops use steel benches for durability and ease of cleaning. You can lay down stainless or galvanized steel as a work surface over wood, which gives you a more durable surface.

containers for parts and label them accordingly.

Clutch friction discs and steels must mate with precision smoothness. Sliding valves must glide through the valve body smoothly. Servo pistons and seals must be clean. These parts will bind if dirty because tolerances are extremely tight to provide proper containment of hydraulic pressure. Seals can also be damaged by dirt and friction material, which causes internal hydraulic leaks, line pressure loss, and malfunction. When you're not working on your transmission, keep it bagged inside a large plastic trash bag.

Tools, Supplies and Equipment

You will need a variety of tools, supplies, and equipment to work

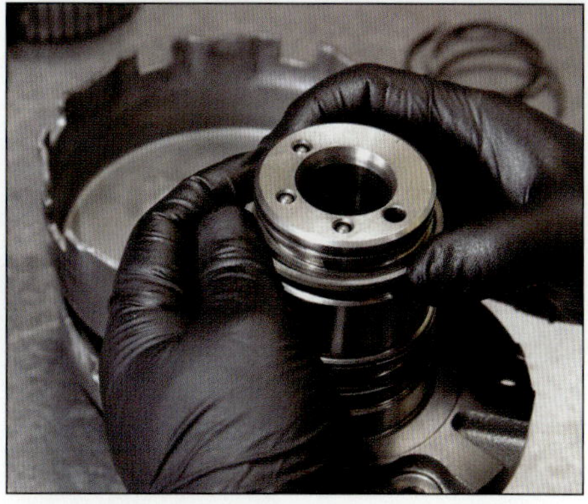

Personal protection is very important to your safety because the risk of injury never takes a day off. Eyes, ears, face, and hands must always be protected. Hazardous cleaning solvents and transmission fluid are why you need to wear protective gloves. Although fluid may seem harmless, there are additives and fallout from use that pose health hazards most of us have never thought of.

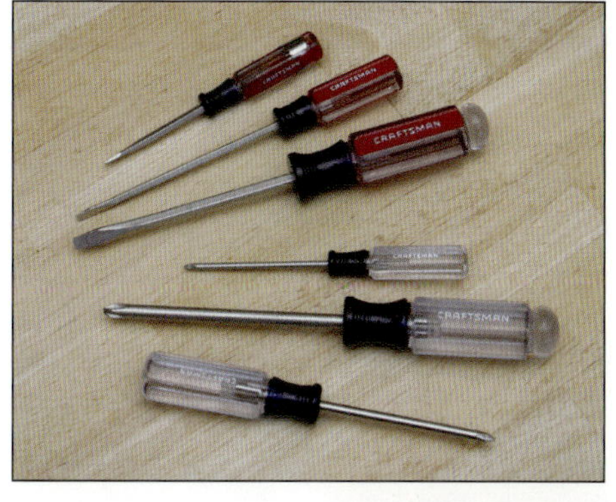

Your tool crib should include most basic hand tools such as screwdrivers of all sizes. Sears Craftsman offers the greatest value for your tool dollar, including a lifetime warranty good just about anywhere in the world. Other sources, such as Harbor Freight, offer specialty tools and equipment for not much money.

You want precision measuring tools such as calipers and micrometers to measure clutch steels, bore diameter, and a host of other dimensions. Because automatic transmissions are all about math and precision assembly, you must understand practical application if you're going to do it yourself.

You will want the full complement of SAE and Metric open and box-end wrenches as well as complete Metric and SAE sockets. Because the AOD/AODE/4R70W transmissions are all Metric designs, Metric is key here.

This clutch piston spring compressor is a transmission shop mainstay because professionals use them every day. However, you can do this at home with three or four C-clamps and get the same result. Remember to use eye and face protection.

It's always good to keep a complete SAE/Metric tap and die set on hand for unexpected surprises. It's also a good idea to keep a set of bolt extractors on hand as well. When you have a bare core, chase all bolt-hole threads for accurate torque readings when it's time for assembly. Examine all bolt and hole threads as well.

A torque wrench must be used on all phases of assembly, primarily in-lbs with automatic transmissions. Never use a torque wrench to loosen fasteners. If you're using a break-away torque wrench, always zero the adjustment after use. It is good to torque fasteners in one-third increments, then check all at least one additional time. Bolt threads should be lubricated with transmission fluid before tightening.

You need both in-lbs and ft-lbs torque wrenches on hand for assembly purposes. And never get the two mixed up. Some Ford Shop manuals have torque table errors you must pay strict attention to. If the torque specification doesn't sound right to you, it probably isn't. Always double-check.

An arbor press or hydraulic press makes light work of bushing and seal installation. Most machine shops have presses.

You may need specialized tools. This is a front pump/shaft removal tool for all kinds of automatics. You may also use a slide hammer if you can get a grip on the input shaft. These tools can be rented.

TRC uses a 7/8-inch wrench as a pry tool to remove servo pistons (shown). There's undoubtedly a specialized tool for this purpose, but why spend the money?

Expect to need all kinds of specialized pliers: needle-nose, duckbill, and more. Because there are many types of C-clips and rings throughout an AOD, you're also going to need a complete set of snap-ring pliers.

Seal installation tools take all forms. The key is to avoid damaging the seals during piston and shaft installation. Here's one approach to seal protection during clutch piston installation using an old thickness gauge.

Transmission shops generally have piston/seal installation tools that make installation easier. However, if you're going to do this only once, why would you buy one? An old set of thickness gauges or even a butter knife can be effective to finesse seals into place.

This Lip Wizard from TransTec is used at TRC, which worked very well for installing clutch pistons and seals. The Lip Wizard is available from any transmission parts supply house.

You will need a complete set of punches of all sizes. Go with high-carbon steel punches, which cost more but are worth every penny. Cheap punches accomplish nothing, and they can cause injury.

A speed handle makes disassembly and assembly easy. Who has time for a ratchet? It is recommended that you use air tools for disassembly but never assembly. Always hand-tighten fasteners before using a torque wrench.

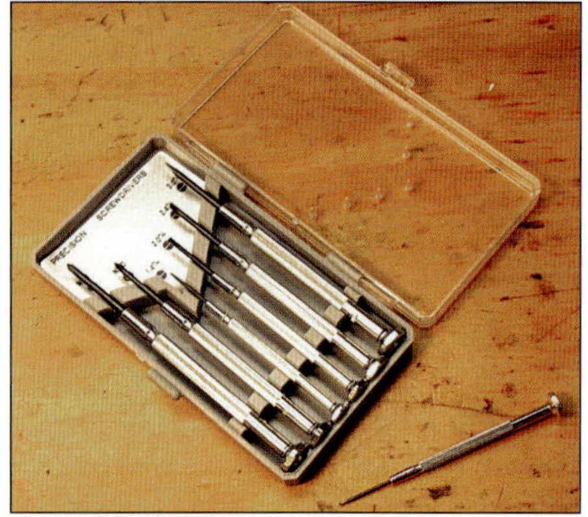

Jeweler's screwdrivers are worth their weight in gold and very effective for working on small items such as valve bodies and roller clutches. You can find jeweler's screwdrivers at any tool supply or home improvement store.

A variety of ball-peen and body hammer sizes should be standard protocol in your toolbox as they can serve many purposes. A set of body dollies should accompany hammers for straightening distorted transmission pans or torque converter covers.

Don't be caught without seal and bushing drivers, which are affordable and available from tool supply and home improvement stores. Seal and bushing drivers prevent installation damage.

Tool Checklist

Although automatic transmission building calls for specialized tools, most of the tools you will need are simple hand tools that you can buy from Harbor Freight, Sears, Snap-on, MAC Tools, Lowe's, and Home Depot. Here's a good basic list of what you will need to buy:

- Combination Wrench Set, SAE and Metric
- 1/4-inch-drive Deep- and Shallow-Well Socket Set, SAE and Metric
- 3/8-inch-drive Deep- and Shallow-Well Socket Set, SAE and Metric
- 1/2-inch-drive Deep- and Shallow-Well Socket Set, SAE and Metric
- 3/8-inch-drive Speed Handle
- 3/8-inch-drive Breaker Bar
- Socket extensions of various lengths and sizes
- Common and Phillips Screwdrivers (all sizes)
- Awl and Pick Set
- Mallet
- Ball-Peen Hammer
- Punch Set
- Tap and Die Set
- Thread Chaser
- Pliers
- Needle-Nose Pliers
- Duckbill Pliers
- Snap-Ring Pliers Set
- Channel Locks
- Vise-Grips
- Putty Knife
- Wire Brush
- C-Clamps (they work just as well as a clutch pack assembly fixture)
- 55-Gallon Trash Bags (dust covers)
- High-Capacity Drain Pan
- Floor Jack or Transmission Jack
- Large-Capacity Jack Stands

You'll need to rent the following:

- 3/8-inch-drive Torque Wrench (ft/lbs)
- 1/4-inch-drive Torque Wrench (in-lbs)
- 3/8-inch-drive Torque Wrench (in-lbs and ft-lbs)
- Transmission-Holding Fixture ■

Although a piece of equipment such as this is probably too expensive for your home workshop, it's good to know a transmission shop that has one. The Hot Flush system pressure surges in two directions to flush out your transmission cooler and lines. It also flushes out transmissions. The Hot Flush system is very effective at removing all damaging debris from your transmission's fluid cooling system.

It's always good to have a parts washer at your convenience to remove heavy grime. If you don't have a parts washer, most machine shops offer parts-cleaning service and hand you components that are clean and ready for assembly.

on your AOD transmission. Some of these items can be rented, especially if you intend to do this only once. You may need to buy others. In some cases, you already have a common household item that can be used.

Most professional transmission shops have transmission-holding fixtures to support transmission cases during disassembly and assembly. Not many of us can afford such a fixture or will even need it again. However, equipment like this can be found at auctions, eBay, Craigslist, and other sources. If you can't find one, you're going to need a hard work surface on which to build your AOD. Although you might think you need a holding fixture, it really isn't necessary for the home garage technician.

Transmission disassembly and assembly get tricky when in the "stack" position, which is standing the transmission on end at the tailshaft end when it's time to load components. Transmission shops generally use tailshaft housings as holding fixtures and have been doing so for decades. If that's not possible, you can always bore a hole in your workbench for vertical assembly. Tool supply houses and home improvement stores offer inexpensive general-purpose holding fixtures designed for most transmission types that work well for disassembly and assembly.

Rebuilding any automatic transmission requires compressed air to clear debris and check servo/clutch pistons for proper function. It's also necessary for the removal of parts such as clutch pistons and sliding valves. During assembly, compressed air is used to check component function. A huge industrial compressor is not required; a 10- to 30-gallon portable compressor that operates off 110/115/120 volts provides plenty of volume. Getting 220 for the more powerful compressors isn't always easy.

Air tools make transmission building faster and easier. A 1/4- and 3/8-inch-drive air wrench and ratchet are sufficient for the job; a 1/2-inch-drive air ratchet would be overkill for automatic transmission repair. If you use an air grinder, take extra care not to damage cast-aluminum contact surfaces. Use air tools for disassembly, but never use them for assembly. Use a torque wrench on every fastener.

Because automatic transmissions have dozens of tiny parts, organization is very important. Use small disposable kitchen containers and mark them for identification purposes. Magnetic parts trays are also a good idea. Baking sheets work well for larger parts such as fasteners, and the sheets can be re-used.

Old-fashioned metal coffee cans are great for cleaning parts. Petroleum-based solvents are a good choice because they minimize the risk of rust and corrosion and make excellent grease cutters. Once the heavy crud is gone, lacquer thinner and brake cleaner are best for final prep work because they have a high evaporation rate.

For items such as the main transmission case, tailshaft housing, and bellhousing, dishwashing detergent and a high-pressure washer work very well. A pressure washer can be rented for a modest fee. Use a pressure washer and compressed air to cleanse and clear passages.

Although hammers are commonplace, a hard mallet is handy for items such as servo covers and pistons. A mallet provides passive-aggressive force without inflicting damage. Forcing any component into place is

This transmission-holding fixture at Tom's Transmissions provides good support and ease of access because it is designed exclusively for this purpose. It can be articulated in nearly any direction.

This portable transmission stand, which is basically an engine stand, is used for transmission assembly at Transmission Rebuilding Company (TRC). Stand mobility makes light work of transmission assembly because you can move it around as needed. Most industrial tool supply houses have transmission-assembly fixtures. Engine stands can be found at speed shops and industrial tool supply houses.

Although many transmission builders build transmissions horizontally on a workbench, the easiest way to assemble a transmission is to "stack build," with the case standing vertically, tailshaft end down, once the tailshaft is installed.

usually cause for concern. Although servo covers and pistons must have a snug fit, installation by force means something's too tight or seals and parts have not been properly lubricated.

Transmission work calls for specialized tools depending upon the type of transmission you are building. You may need to modify snap-ring pliers to get at certain snap rings in your AOD/AODE/4R70W. Although clutch piston return spring compression tools are the best to use, you can use C-clamps instead, which are available at any hardware store.

As mentioned earlier, some tools must be purchased to do the job properly. Teflon seal installation tools are a must-have. Bushing removal requires the appropriate tool or tool modification to drive a bushing out. A slide caliper is necessary to measure steels and frictions. Simple tools can be modified or fabricated, such as long headless bolts to make front pump installation easier with less chance of seal damage. You can make a pick from a common screwdriver by heating and bending the tip; this can be accomplished with a variety of screwdrivers.

Transmission Removal

To rebuild an AOD-, AODE-, or 4R70W-series transmission, you must first remove it from the vehicle. Because you want a clean job with a minimum of fuss, drain all fluids from the transmission sump and torque converter. Allow the fluid to drain overnight with the pan removed if you can. Disconnect the cooler lines and allow them to drain. Always recycle old, dirty fluid responsibly.

Whenever you rebuild or replace an automatic transmission, you should replace all transmission cooler lines and, if possible, the cooler, to eliminate any chance of debris damaging the fresh transmission.

Transmission removal should begin with safe vehicle support: large-capacity jack stands in all four corners that can get the vehicle high enough for you to work freely underneath. Never trust your life to a hydraulic jack and never jack on an incline. A floor jack or low-profile transmission jack can be used for removal and installation. To ensure your safety, it is best never to undertake transmission removal and installation alone.

To save time, determine what you will need and make sure you have the appropriate tools before getting started. Few things are more frustrating than being underneath a vehicle only to have to make several trips to the toolbox.

Jack Stands

If you are removing an AOD on a garage floor or flat driveway, always support the vehicle with heavy-duty jack stands. Use stands that are large enough to support a 1-ton pickup truck to get the vehicle high enough in the air to allow you to move around. Ideally, there should be 24 inches between the rocker panel and the floor. Position the jack stands at the frame rails in all four corners. ■

Prepare for Removal

1 Remove Items in the Way

Transmission removal normally begins with items that tend to get in the way, such as exhaust systems, wiring, and parking brake cables. H-pipe assemblies are normally easy to remove unless they have been welded together. This 1993 Mustang GT has a bolt-on Flowmaster cat-back H-pipe.

2 Remove Crossmember

Once the transmission is properly supported, the crossmember is unbolted and removed. This is the time to replace the crossmember bushings and mount along with anything else time and mileage may have worn.

3 Remove Driveshaft

On the driveshaft, make reference marks at the flange and yoke so you can reinstall them in the same position with the reference marks aligned. This is the time to have the driveshaft rebuilt and balanced with new universal joints and a slip yoke. The driveshaft should be checked by a professional for run-out and any stress issues.

Professional Mechanic Tip

PRO TIP

4 Disconnect Accessories

PRO TIP Disconnect the shift linkages and TV cable. Note the TV cable adjustment and installation before disassembly. Do the same with the cable manual-shift linkage.

5 Remove Exhaust Heat Shield

Next, remove the heat shield, which makes the transmission easier to remove. The heat shield is there to keep extreme catalytic converter heat away. Reuse this heat shield when it's time for installation.

6 Disconnect Battery and Remove Starter

Disconnect the battery's negative cable, then remove the starter. This is a reduction-gear Denso starter, common from 1992-up. The smaller trigger lead fires the solenoid in this application. Before 1991, expect to see a Motorcraft light-duty starter.

7 Remove Bellhousing and Dust Shield

Remove the torque converter/flexplate dust shield, which reveals the converter-to-flexplate studs and locknuts. There are four locknuts. It is a good idea to replace the locknuts with new ones. You can access all four nuts by rotating the engine manually.

8 Disconnect Flexplate and Torque Converter

Remove the flexplate locknuts to free up the transmission and torque converter. During installation, use a good thread locker, along with new locknuts.

Important!

9 Disconnect Cooler Lines

Disconnect the transmission cooler lines. Even if your transmission didn't fail, the lines and cooler must be flushed or replaced. Debris such as clutch and band friction material and metal can become trapped in the lines and cooler and damage the new transmission.

10 Unbolt Bellhousing and Lower Transmission

Most applications call for a 5/8-inch socket to remove the bellhousing bolts. Most bolts can be removed from underneath. You may have to use a box-end wrench to remove the top two bolts, depending upon firewall clearances.

11 Inspect Flexplate

The flexplate should be inspected for cracks, proper installation, and ring gear damage. The starter drive should also be inspected. While you're under there, look for rear main seal and pan gasket leakage on the engine. This is the time to correct any problems before reassembly.

12 Prepare for Teardown

After you remove the AOD, it is ready for teardown. Teardown is an opportunity to learn why transmission failure, if any, occurred. It is also a chance to examine wear patterns that could cause problems in the future.

13 Remove and Inspect Electrical Components

All fittings, switches, and sensors should be removed at this time. The transmission case should be stripped completely bare for cleaning. If you're performing a transmission build at home, have all of the parts professionally cleaned or, at the least, pressure washed with a good solvent. This is something you can do at home, especially if you're on a tight budget.

AOD Disassembly

Rebuilding an AOD, AODE, or 4R70W has always been perceived as a task for professionals only. And for the most part, it is best left to them, especially if you lack the confidence necessary to do it yourself. However, if you really want to understand automatic transmission function, you can perform the rebuild at home.

Follow this book carefully, pay close attention to all the details, and you can achieve great success rebuilding your Ford AOD. The key here is to take sharp, well-focused images and liberal notes during each phase of disassembly.

Why Transmissions Fail

Disassembly is a forensics study to learn why a transmission failed and how to prevent failure from happening again. Some transmission rebuilds are nothing more than attending to wear and tear. However, most are failure related.

Fundamentally, the AOD is a simple automatic because it employs the same basic core as the cast-iron FMX with its Ravigneaux compound planetaries. The main difference is the addition of an overdrive system and throttle valve modulation.

In general, not enough attention is paid to regular preventative maintenance: fluid and filter changes. Automatic transmissions, regardless of automakers' claims of "life of the unit" service intervals, require regular fluid and filter changes every 30,000 miles for maximum longevity. Yet most motorists never give it a thought until they're on the roadside, waiting for a flatbed.

Clean, plentiful lubrication is crucial to long life. Clean lubrication provides a good oil wedge between moving parts and good hydraulic line pressure via healthy seals and clutch discs. Clutch and band frictions saturated with plenty of fluid go the distance and provide durability.

There's a long-standing belief that if a transmission has never been serviced it is best to leave well enough alone and let it run its course until failure or a rebuild. Most transmission professionals have indicated that fresh fluid tends to shock old seals, leading to pressure loss and failure. These same professionals also say that transmission failure can depend upon how abused the transmission has been along the way. Towing and competition cause heat damage to seals and clutches. If your transmission has passed the 100,000-mile mark in normal operation without a fluid change, it is best to leave well enough alone until it requires a rebuild.

Burned Clutches and Bands

Brian Fortune of Tom's Transmissions suggests that as you disassemble an AOD, AODE, or 4R70W, it is important to first determine failure origin. Failure isn't always the first thing you see; it may be something seemingly unrelated that indirectly caused the failure. This could be a loss of line pressure from a worn seal, a sticking pressure relief valve, or dirty fluid, any of which may explain why clutches and bands burned up. Clutches and bands burn due to slippage and no other reason, aside from fluid starvation.

Transmission failure is normally a chain reaction, according to Brian; a series of small issues and disruptions that lead to failure. The normal pattern of failure is seal wear or damage, which leads to loss of hydraulic pressure and clutch and band slippage. This in turn contaminates the fluid with friction material, cutting seals and further hindering control pressure, causing slippage and burned clutch and band frictions.

Poor Assembly

Transmissions also fail due to poor assembly technique in transmission shops, according to Mike Stewart of Mike's Transmission. Whether it is the mass rebuilder or an independent repair shop, he believes that many things are overlooked in the course of a transmission rebuild.

During teardown, you want to study wear patterns and anything else that appears out of the ordinary. Look for parts that don't work well together. Just because the transmission functioned doesn't mean it was assembled properly. Mass rebuilders, for example, toss thousands of parts in bins with other seemingly like parts, clean them up, machine or replace as necessary, and put transmissions together haphazardly. The result is different generations of transmission parts thrown together that aren't always engineered to work well together.

Factory Engineering Changes

Ford is notorious for making engineering changes, and dozens of them occur over the production life of a transmission design. This means you must pay very close attention to parts intended to work together as well as parts that were never designed to be together. The AOD, for example, had significant changes throughout its production life, which means you can wind up with parts that don't even fit, let alone work well together. Teardown teaches us what went wrong with a transmission: it also provides the opportunity to learn how it should go back together. Take plenty of pictures and liberal notes as you go along. When something just doesn't look right, take note of it and don't be afraid to ask questions.

Examine for Heat Damage

Look for discoloration and damage to even the smallest parts. A bluish color on steel parts indicates extreme heat (slippage), especially with steel clutch plates. Burned steel clutch plates should be discarded. Burned steels lose temper and can crack. It is risky to reuse them. ■

Begin Disassembly

1 Remove Pan and Filter

Disassembly begins with removing the pan and filter. The pan has 14 bolts and the filter has three. The first order of business is to examine the remaining transmission fluid in the sump. If it's brown to black in color, this indicates badly burned friction bands and clutches, which normally happens due to a loss of control pressure. Insufficient pressure causes clutch and band slippage and the corresponding heat.

Important!

2 Unbolt Valve Body

Remove the valve body using a 10-mm socket; it should be completely disassembled for cleaning. Use a digital camera to record how it comes apart. Closely examine all moving parts (valves and balls) for damage/scoring.

3 Remove Valve Body

Carefully remove the valve body and lay it on the bench with the separator plate facing up. Because there are ball check valves throughout the valve body, it must be flat on the bench to avoid losing these critical parts.

4 Examine Manual and Throttle Valves

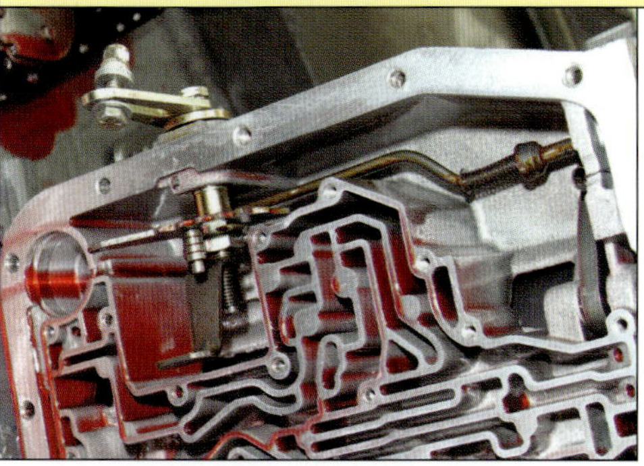

The manual and throttle valve mechanisms are exposed once you remove the valve body. The manual/throttle valve linkage is a shaft within a hollow shaft configuration. The manual shaft is hollow, and the throttle valve shaft is solid within the manual shaft.

Tailshaft, Servos and Pistons Removal

1 Remove Tailshaft Housing

When removing the tailshaft housing pay attention to the seal and bushing condition. Both must be replaced in the course of a rebuild. Go with a new bushing, seal, and slip yoke. This is a transmission shop with work-bench drains. At home, you need to have completely drained the transmission or you will have a huge mess. Make sure the transmission is completely drained first.

2 Remove Overdrive Band Servo

Remove the overdrive band servo cover and piston assembly using a common screwdriver to get at the snap ring. This snap ring can be tricky to remove. You may also use two small common screwdrivers or an awl for snap-ring removal.

Critical Inspection

3 Inspect Overdrive Band Servo Piston

Remove the overdrive cover/piston assembly and take a close look at seals and the bore for scoring. Seal and/or bore damage is caused by fluid contamination. Fluid contamination can be caused by clutch/band friction material, which only gets worse with time and slippage. Scoring can be honed out of the bore. Piston scoring calls for replacement.

4 Remove Low-Reverse Servo Cover

The low-reverse servo cover assembly is next. Using a common screwdriver, remove the snap ring. Push on the cover/piston with a hammer handle or your thumb to relieve the pressure on the snap ring.

5 Remove Low-Reverse Servo Piston

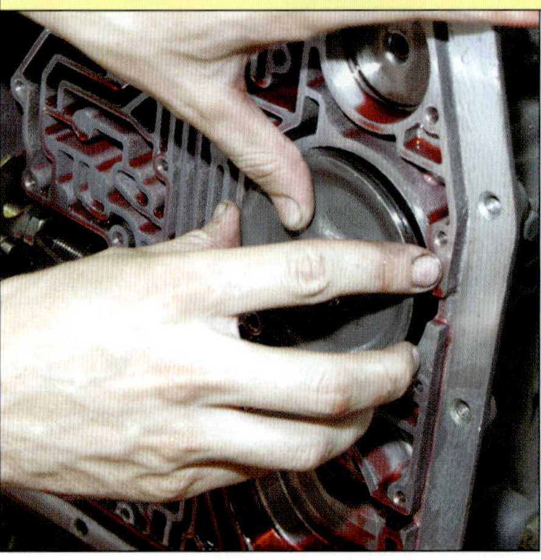

This is the low-reverse servo cover and snap ring. The piston and return ring are inside the low-reverse servo bore. Inspect the piston seal and bore for damage, especially if there's fluid contamination.

6 Remove 2-3 Shift Accumulator

The 2-3 accumulator cover (next to the low-reverse servo) is next, with snap-ring removal. Again, look for signs of leakage and bore damage issues.

7 Inspect 2-3 Shift Accumulator Piston

The 2-3 accumulator piston has two seals. Inspect the seal and bore condition. Any scoring or seal damage is a clue to what may have happened to control pressure.

Front Pump Removal and Disassembly

1 Pull Front Pump Assembly

Using a puller, remove the front pump assembly, which is iron in the AOD and aluminum in the AODE and 4R70W. Not all applications require a puller. But count on needing one to get the pump out.

2 Inspect Front Pump Assembly

The AOD front pump assembly also includes the intermediate clutch piston and spring retainer assembly. The spring retainer returns the intermediate clutch piston to rest when pressure is released. The intermediate clutch pack is at the front of the case.

3 Remove Intermediate Clutch Piston

Remove the intermediate clutch piston from the pump housing, which is also the clutch cylinder. Inspect the seal and bore for scoring and damage. The three domes (or bumps) in each of the three sections are return spring mounts.

4 Disassemble Front Pump

Split the front pump housing by removing the five fine-thread bolts with a 10-mm socket. This is also the intermediate clutch cylinder sans piston.

5 Inspect Front Pump Cavity

With the front pump opened up, the AOD's gear pump main cavity is ready for inspection. Before removing the rotating assembly, examine the inner and outer gears for unusual wear patterns and scoring. Also inspect the pump cavity walls for scoring.

Internal Components Removal and Inspection

1 Pull Forward Rotating Assembly

With the pump removed, the input shaft, intermediate clutch, one-way clutch, reverse clutch, and forward clutch come out as an assembly.

2 Inspect Low-Reverse Drum

This is the intermediate clutch pressure plate and forward rotating assembly just removed from the main case. Examine the low-reverse clutch drum (also known as the overdrive drum) for excessive wear and tear. Make plans now to go with the wider Lincoln drum and overdrive band.

3 Examine Intermediate Clutches and Plates

Inspect the intermediate clutches and clutch plates for abnormal wear patterns. As with any rebuild, replace the clutch discs and dress the steel plates. Check the steel plates for heat cracking and discoloring.

4 Separate Low-Reverse Clutch from Forward Clutch

Separate the low-reverse clutch drum from the forward clutch. Check the clutch hubs for scoring and damage. Look for atypical wear patterns, such as shiny spots and nicks that can snag clutches. Normal wear patterns are uniform in nature.

5 Examine Low-Reverse Clutches

Give the low-reverse clutch discs and steel plates a close look for excessive and unusual wear such as general discoloration, hot spots, and cracking. These clutch discs and plates look good and can be returned to service. However, the clutch plates should always be replaced. The steel plates can be resurfaced.

Critical Inspection

6 Check Wear Patterns

Inspect the low-reverse clutch shim for abnormal wear. There doesn't appear to be any unusual wear patterns here, which means the shim can be returned to service.

7 Remove Clutch Hub

Remove the intermediate clutch hub from the low-reverse clutch pack. Inspect it closely for wear and damage. The clutch hub teeth must be smooth so clutch frictions can move freely.

8 Inspect Low-Reverse One-Way Clutch

This is the low-reverse drum's one-way roller clutch, which allows rotation one way, but not the other. Rollers and springs should be free of damage and missing parts. If there's any doubt, or even minor scoring, replace the one-way clutch.

9 Examine Low-Reverse Drum

This is the low-reverse drum in a disassembled state, revealing the wavy Belleville spring inside the clutch drum, which releases this clutch pack. The interior clutch disc teeth should be free of scoring and any irregularity that would hinder clutch movement.

10 Disassemble Forward Clutch

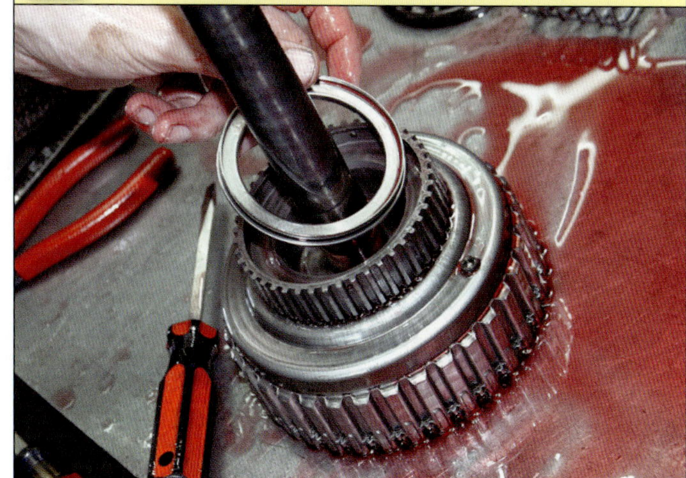

Disassemble the forward clutch, including the Torrington bearing and clutch hub. Inspect the teeth for scoring and any damage that can hinder clutch friction movement.

11 Remove Overdrive Band

With the low-reverse drum and forward clutch removed, the overdrive band is next. To make your AOD the best it can be in terms of durability, opt for the wider 2-inch Lincoln overdrive band and corresponding drum for greater hookup. Never reuse the overdrive band.

12 Inspect Forward Clutch Hub

Inspect the forward clutch hub for irregularities that can cause clutch friction issues. The teeth should be free of scoring that can hinder clutch movement.

13 Remove Drive Shell and Sun Gear

Remove the drive shell and forward sun gear, again with close inspection of gear teeth for abnormal wear patterns. Look at the shell's central hub and check for cracks.

14 Remove Center Support and Planet Carrier

Remove the center support and planet carrier. Pay close attention to the anti-clunk spring during this phase of disassembly as it's easy to overlook.

Documentation Required

15 Inspect Planet Carrier

Disassemble and inspect the planet carrier. The planet gears should spin freely and be free of side play (wobble). Any resistance or binding is cause for rejection. This is the planet carrier's one-way roller clutch assembly. It should be replaced, but if you feel compelled to reuse it, inspect all of the rollers and springs. Note the assembly position for proper installation of rollers and springs.

16 Remove Low-Reverse Band

Remove the low-reverse band. The low-reverse band, which is cast iron with a friction surface, doesn't work as hard as the overdrive band and as a rule rarely has to be replaced. Regardless, it's always a good idea to start with a fresh low-reverse band to minimize the risk of failure, especially on a high-mileage transmission.

Disassembly

The proper path to take during transmission teardown begins with draining and appropriately recycling fluid and worn parts. Remove the pan first and examine the sump for contaminated fluid. Pink fluid indicates stability and proper operation. Burned fluid results from high operating temperatures; a lot of friction material in the fluid indicates clutch and band slippage.

Geartrain Removal

Once the pan is removed and you have access to the valve body, keep close track of bolt size and length during valve body removal. With the valve body removed, you have access to servo pistons, the accumulator, manual and throttle valve linkages, and the parking pawl. Before disassembling the linkages, take pictures and notes.

Tailshaft housing removal reveals the governor on AOD models. (AODE and 4R70W models do not have a governor.) Governor disassembly requires great care and is something that needs to be done separately because disassembly and assembly are performed all in one process. Lay the governor out as assembled and take pictures just in case. Governors are calibrated based on vehicle type and load.

Servos and accumulators (2-3 and 3-4), which are retained with snap rings and covers, are removed next. Not all AOD units have the 3-4 shift accumulator, which was discontinued in 1989. The overdrive band servo has a snap ring, cast-aluminum cover, and piston. The low-reverse servo has a snap ring, steel cover, and piston. As you remove these assemblies, examine the seals for damage and the hard parts for scoring. Check the springs for integrity. If there's any doubt, replace the spring.

When the servos have been removed from the case, this frees up the geartrain. The front pump is removed using a puller because it is such a tight fit. An AOD uses a cast-iron pump and stator support; because iron and aluminum are dissimilar metals, this combination can prove challenging. The AODE and 4R70W pumps are aluminum, which tend to be easier to remove by hand. Never beat the pump/stator with a hammer. Gently pry where you can. If the pump proves to be stubborn, use a puller. You can also use a slide hammer, which is easier to find at a rental outlet.

After you have removed the pump and inner overdrive input shaft, the geartrain slides out in segments. First to come out is the intermediate clutch pack, one-way clutch, forward clutch, and hub. Carefully remove the overdrive band and examine the friction material for wear and tear. It should be replaced regardless of condition. Turn the overdrive band to get it off the anchor pin and remove. Next comes the sun gear and number-5 Torrington (thrust) bearing.

With the forwardmost portion of the geartrain out, next is the support assembly, which is locked in place with a large snap ring and buffered with anti-clunk springs. Pay close attention to how the support assembly is positioned. The support assembly comes out with the planet carrier. Remember to take pictures as you go. Next, remove the low-reverse band.

Next in line are the direct clutch, steels, and frictions, which are tied to the output shaft. Because the governor has already been removed, the output shaft should slide out through the front of the transmission case. With all rotational assemblies removed, you will see the number-9 Torrington (thrust) bearing, which is removed at this time.

Washers and Bearings

Closely examine thrust washers and Torrington bearings for excessive heat and abnormal wear. Thrust washers act as thrust bushings between rotating assemblies to control endplay and act as a bearing surface. Torrington bearings are low-friction needle bearing assemblies that act as thrusts between rotating assemblies. A good practice is to replace thrusts and Torrington bearings at every rebuild. ■

Governor Removal

If you remove the governor assembly with the front of the case pointed downward, the output shaft will fall out and hit the floor. Make sure the case is pointed sideways or straight up when removing the output shaft. Disassemble and inspect the governor as a separate step before moving on. This is crucial because the governor consists of a number of very small precision parts. Disassemble and lay these parts out in the order they come out of the governor. Only the AOD has a mechanical governor on the output shaft. The AODE and 4R70W are computer controlled and are not equipped with a mechanical governor. ■

Governor and Output Shaft Removal

1 Remove Governor Assembly

To remove the governor valve remove the C-clip. Governors are calibrated for vehicle type and weight by spring pressure. If your AOD is being installed into the same vehicle that it originally came from (or a similar vehicle), you should have few concerns about governor calibration.

However, if your AOD core is from an unknown vehicle, it would be wise to calibrate the governor to your application, using the spring combination shown in the Ford Master Parts Catalog for your particular vehicle type. The governor controls are based on output shaft speed, which controls line pressure.

2 Remove Governor Drive Ball

The governor valve is driven by the output shaft and this ball, which acts like a Woodruff key. Do not lose this ball. Keep it in a safe place for reassembly.

3 Remove Direct Clutch and Output Shaft

Completely disassemble the direct clutch and output shaft package, right down to where the output shaft joins the direct clutch. Debris can become trapped in the clutch drum and contaminate the fluid.

4 Disassemble Direct Clutch and Output Shaft

Disassembling the direct clutch and output shaft exposes the number-8 Torrington thrust bearing. All cast-iron and Teflon shaft seals should be removed, taking note of their positions and the type of seal.

Critical Inspection

5 Inspect Direct Clutch

Disassemble the direct clutch to reveal clutches and steels. Inspect the clutch discs and plates for heat issues and scoring. As has been stressed earlier, clutch discs must be replaced and the plates inspected for heat damage and wear.

6 Inspect and Resurface Plates

These clutch discs and plates look healthy, although the plates could use some help. When the plates are shiny, they can be resurfaced to a healthy crosshatch pattern for good clutch hookup.

Subassembly Removal

With the geartrain removed, the subassemblies must be disassembled. The reverse clutch pack (also known as the overdrive drum) and forward clutch are disassembled next. Keep track of the number of clutches and steels in each of the clutch packs. As clutches and steels come out, inspect both for abnormal wear. Any bluing in the steels is cause for rejection and further investigation to learn why they became hot.

Most transmission rebuild kits come with fresh steels and clutches, which means you won't be using the originals. If you're going to reuse steels, reface them with a very fine abrasive in a swirling motion to promote good clutch hookup. You do not want shiny clutch steels, but instead rough surfaces for better engagement.

While you have the geartrain disassembled, inspect the one-way clutch (reverse clutch drum) for smooth, consistent operation. It should turn smoothly in one direction, but lock up in the opposite. Any inconsistencies are cause for rejection and replacement.

Each clutch drum has an apply piston, which engages the clutches and steels. Pistons are generally removed with compressed air. When doing this, turn the clutch drum down, away from your face, and pop the piston toward the workbench and a soft towel to prevent damage. Inspect the inner and outer piston seals for damage that may have caused transmission malfunction.

Each clutch pack must be carefully inspected for areas that can cause clutch frictions and steels to hang up. Ragged edges and scored surfaces should be checked with clutches and steels in place to see how these segments function. If they hang up, dress the irregular surface or replace the drum.

The front pump assembly is also the intermediate clutch cylinder and piston, which is disassembled, cleaned, and inspected. Look for irregularities such as unusual wear, ragged edges, and scoring that can damage clutch piston seals. Make sure all return springs are present and serviceable.

When you split the pump for a look inside, be sure to note how the inner and outer pump gears are configured and carefully remove them for inspection. They must go back in exactly as they came out. Examine the surfaces for scoring and excessive wear. If wear is excessive, replace the pump. You can always replace the gears. If they are worn, however, chances are very good that the pump cavity is also excessively worn.

As you disassemble the clutch drums and other subassemblies, make sure you have removed all seals and bearings/thrusts. Seals, especially, are easy to overlook when they must be replaced.

Soft Parts Replacement

1 Perform a Thorough Cleaning

All transmission hard parts go into a parts washer. Make sure all small parts have been accounted for. When these items come out, dry them with compressed air, which should be blasted into all passages.

2 Replace Broken Belleville Spring

This low-reverse clutch pack has a cracked Belleville spring, which must be replaced. This is a stress crack due to metal cyclic fatigue. Belleville springs work in a fashion called "oil canning." In time, the metal weakens and cracks due to duty cycling back and forth as pressure is applied to the clutch piston. Play it safe and replace all Belleville springs during a rebuild.

3 Replace Overdrive Band

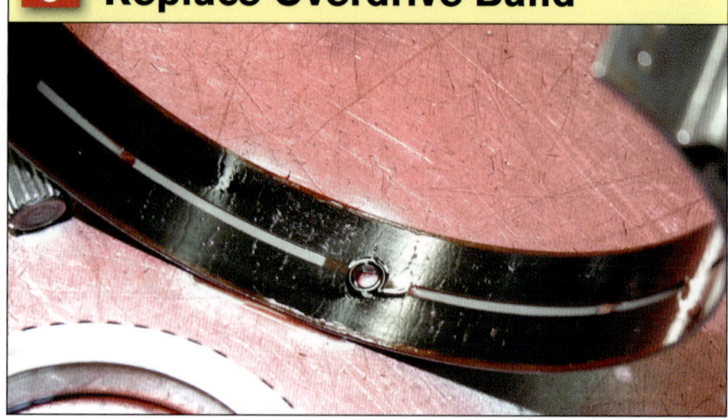

Here's another look at a burned overdrive band with heat cracking in the friction. Regardless of the condition, overdrive bands must always be replaced and the drum dressed for good hookup without slippage.

Precision Measurement

4 Inspect Low-Reverse Band

The low-reverse band is different from the overdrive band; it's cast iron with friction material instead of steel. The low-reverse band isn't subjected to as much stress as the overdrive band and lasts considerably longer. Replacement is suggested in any case.

5 Use C-Clamps for Clutch Disassembly

Although transmission shops often have clutch spring compressors for piston and clutch removal, you can do this at home with C-clamps. Be sure to always use eye and face protection.

6 Remove All Seals

With each clutch drum disassembly, make sure you remove all the seals and take note of the seal type and location during disassembly. Installing seals backward and in the wrong location is common and can cost you plenty in terms of time and money.

7 Replace All Seals

Some piston seals are well hidden, which means you need to examine every square inch of a clutch piston and drum during disassembly to make sure all seals have been removed. Not all seals are neoprene. Some are iron, Teflon, and other synthetics. They must all be replaced.

AOD Improvements and Assembly

The objective of this chapter is to show you how to improve the AOD's durability and performance with the best parts and improved shift programming. Because the AOD's geartrain is based on the FMX, FX, and MX transmissions, it has proven to be reliable, with generations of refinement leading up to what is now a very rugged transmission.

You can build a durable AOD using upgraded Ford parts from the late 1980s, or you can step up to AODE/4R70W geartrain components that help improve both performance and durability, especially the AOD's weakest link, the reverse drum and overdrive band. There are plenty of AODE/4R70W donor cores out there and a wealth of new aftermarket parts engineered to make your AOD world class.

The AOD is covered separately from the AODE in this book because it really is a different transmission, although the basic fundamentals are the same. If you're building the AOD for performance use, you want AODE/4R70W geartrain components. If you're building an AOD for your daily commute, you can go with original geartrain components and get the desired durability. The choice boils down to how you want the transmission to perform. If you want improved acceleration, you want the 4R70W's geartrain with its wide-ratio 1-2-3-4 upshift.

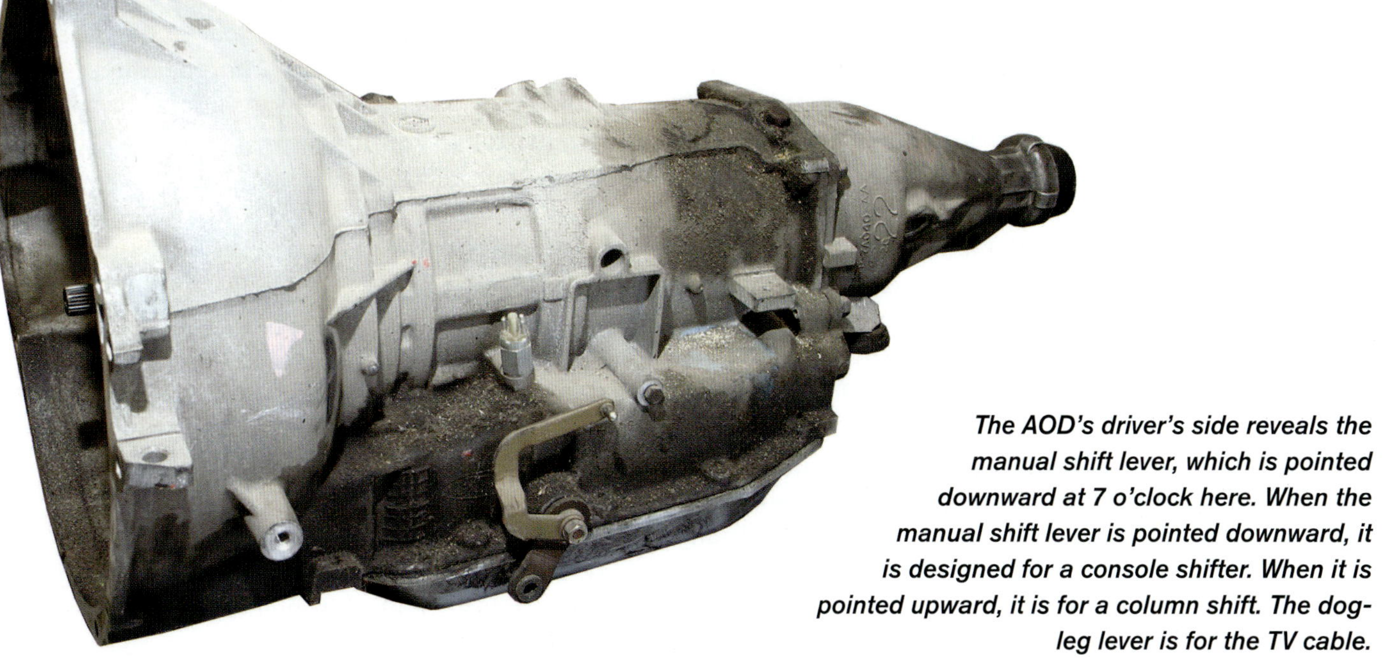

The AOD's driver's side reveals the manual shift lever, which is pointed downward at 7 o'clock here. When the manual shift lever is pointed downward, it is designed for a console shifter. When it is pointed upward, it is for a column shift. The dog-leg lever is for the TV cable.

Operation and Power Flow

AOD operation begins with a six-position shifter marked P-R-N-D(OD)-D-1. These ranges are park, reverse, neutral, drive/overdrive, drive (without overdrive), and first. Beginning in 1991, the AOD couldn't be placed in gear without a foot on the brake pedal.

When the selector is placed in drive/overdrive, a normal 1-2-3-4 upshift pattern occurs, with overdrive/lockup taking place at around 40 mph. The drive/overdrive position is a fully automatic operation. Slip the selector into "D" and you get 1-2-3 upshifts without overdrive or fourth gear. Start out in "1" and you get a 1-2 upshift, but no higher.

As acceleration begins from a stop, fluid under pressure flows through the torque converter in the conventional manner via impeller, stator, and turbine. Anytime the converter is multiplying torque, which happens under all acceleration, however light, fluid temperature increases because there is an increase in pressure and resistance to fluid flow. As fluid temperature increases, viscosity changes and shift quality/function changes.

Fluid under pressure flows first through the outer hollow input shaft during torque multiplication (acceleration and light throttle) and into the geartrain in ranges 1-2-3 and reverse. In overdrive, pressure is channeled from the torque converter shell directly to the overdrive unit via the solid inner shaft, bypassing the torque converter function completely. It feels like a manual transmission in overdrive because there is no slippage or torque multiplication. This process is referred to as "split torque" because fluid flows via torque multiplication (on the torque converter) under acceleration into the geartrain through the smaller input shaft and straight drive when the transmission is in overdrive.

Brian Fortune of Tom's Transmissions sets up a client's AOD, which has already been modified with performance improvements. It is being freshened up with new clutch friction discs, steel plates, and seals, along with AODE/4R70W components from TCI Automotive. Brian makes sure he has clean parts and plenty of transmission assembly lube and fluid on hand before starting.

The Ford AOD is different from most automatic overdrive transmissions because it does not have a locking torque converter. Instead, it has a locking overdrive unit driven by the smaller secondary input shaft within the main input shaft. The AOD also differs in that overdrive isn't an afterthought; it's incorporated into the existing geartrain rather than being a bolt-on. It is a true 4-speed automatic overdrive transmission.

In "D/OD," which is fully automatic, the AOD performs a 1-2-3-4 upshift as vehicle speed increases. At 40 mph, the AOD is designed to shift into overdrive lockup on the smaller input shaft into the direct clutch. There are two types of throttle valve control systems used with the AOD. The 3.8L Essex V-6 and 5.8L (351-ci) Windsor V-8 employ a control-rod throttle valve modulation system without a vacuum modulator. The 5.0L (302-ci) V-8 engine uses a TV cable system.

The throttle valve shift modulation system does what the vacuum modulator and throttle kickdown linkage did with the C4, C6, and FMX transmissions. The throttle valve system controls line pressure and shift-points based on throttle position only.

Internal Components Installation

1 Inspect Kit Parts

A complete AOD overhaul kit from TCI Automotive includes fresh clutch frictions and steel plates, along with gaskets, seals, and a new filter. These items, coupled with AODE/4R70W hard parts such as bearings, bushings, and thrust washers from TCI, make the AOD ready for real power.

2 Install New Bushings and Seals

Install a new bushing and seal in the tailshaft housing. Remember, some seals incorporate a lip spring. Pack wheel bearing grease around the spring to keep it in place during installation.

3 Install Front Pump Seal

Assemble the front pump with a new seal and bushing. The seal should be packed with assembly lube to prevent lip spring loss. The bushing should also receive generous amounts of assembly lube.

4 Fill Pump Cavity with Transmission Fluid

For a good pump prime and plenty of lube, fill the AOD's front pump cavity with transmission fluid. When you fill the pump cavity with solid assembly lube or transmission fluid, you get plenty of lubrication and line pressure with the initial start-up.

5 Orient Pump Gears

The front pump is a gear type, which provides a steady, uninterrupted flow of fluid under pressure. There are two gears: the drive gear (inner) and the driven gear (outer). The inner drive gear must be installed with the open side toward the torque converter. Get this backward and the torque converter does not seat/engage into the pump. The chamfered sides of both gears face into the pump housing.

Torque Fasteners

6 Install Front Pump and Torque Bolts

The back half of the pump housing is mated to the stator support half. Torque the bolts to 12 to 16 ft-lbs. The transmission side of the pump fits only one way.

7 Assemble Intermediate Clutch Cylinder

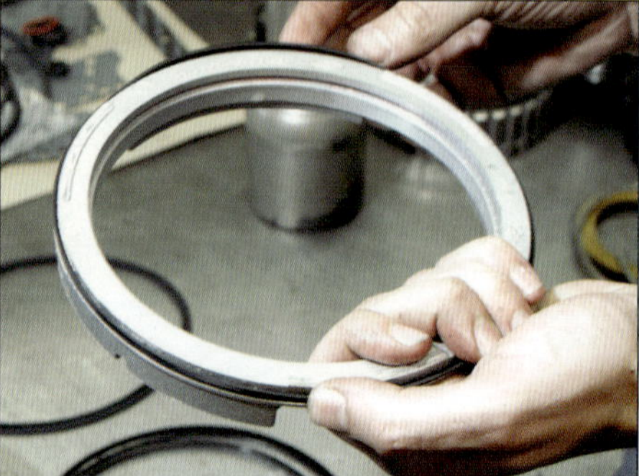

The intermediate clutch piston fits into the pump housing, which doubles as a clutch pack for all those clutches in front. Proper clutch piston seal installation is crucial. Some seals have lips that must be angled where they seal against the piston and bore from the pressure side. Get this backward and it cannot seal.

8 Install Intermediate Clutch Piston

Perform the intermediate clutch piston installation with great care to protect the inner and outer seals. Use a seal lip manipulation tool with a close eye on the seal status. Seal distortion or tearing is unacceptable.

9 Install Front Pump Seal

Use plenty of transmission assembly lube to install the pump perimeter seal. Transmission assembly lube is compatible with transmission fluid. Always use an assembly lubricant that works with transmission fluid.

10 Install Pump Sealing Rings

Carefully install the iron pump seal rings. They are very specific in function and location. The reverse clutch sealing rings are closest to the pump's main cavity. The forward clutch sealing rings are near the end of the clutch support. These rings all contain line pressure much like an engine piston ring contains cylinder pressures. The ends are gapless, which means they interlock.

Important!

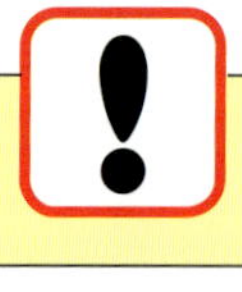

11 Install Forward Clutch Piston Seals

Install the forward clutch piston inner and outer seals with liberal lubrication to prevent seal damage and distortion. The seal lip must be pointed toward the pressure source, away from the clutches to be effective. Get this backward and the seals do not hold pressure.

Special Tool

12 Install Forward Clutch Piston

Use the seal protection tool to install the clutch piston so the seals glide in smoothly. This tool helps prevent seal damage. Other types of installation tools are available. The key to success is watching the clutch seals carefully as you go.

13 Install Forward Clutch Piston Return Springs

Use a C-clip retainer with the clutch piston return spring. This is an AODE/4R70W forward clutch drum, which is stamped steel instead of iron, and it has a single return spring.

14 Load Forward Clutch Frictions and Steels

It's time to load the forward clutch with steels and frictions. Begin with the wavy plate at the clutch piston, then load clutch discs and plates alternately.

15 Install Forward Clutch Steels and Frictions

Install the clutch discs and plates alternately until you arrive at the clutch pressure plate. Soak the clutch discs in transmission fluid before installation as fluid affects clutch thickness and clearances.

16 Check Forward Clutch Clearances

Load the pressure plate after all frictions and steels are in. Clearances should be .050 to .089 inch for V-8s and .040 to .071 inch for V-6s between the pressure plate and the first disc.

17 Choose Snap-Ring Thicknesses

Snap rings of different thicknesses are available from transmission supply houses if clearances are not within specifications. Snap rings are of different thicknesses to yield desired clearances.

Faults and Fixes

The AOD wasn't always as durable as it was near the end of production in the early 1990s. In the beginning, the AOD was prone to failure and didn't tolerate the power of high-performance engines. By 1989, the AOD was on top of its game as a rugged, reliable overdrive thanks to engineering upgrades that made it more dependable. The AOD's weaknesses are as follows:

- The direct clutch didn't have a sufficient number of clutches and steel plates to handle the amount of power Ford put into it with the 5.0L high-output engines that first arrived in the early 1980s.
- The overdrive band and reverse drum weren't wide enough to handle the load because there wasn't enough surface area. Both became wider on later models to better handle the load.
- The AOD had insufficient line pressure to both the direct clutch and overdrive band during hard acceleration. Although it appears to be an engineered failure, it was Ford's intent to reduce pump load and improve fuel economy. Unfortunately, this turn of events occurred at the 2-3 upshift, which caused clutch and band slippage, along with destructive heat.
- Irregular line pressure was hard on both the direct and forward clutches. Line pressure was low when it needed to be high and vice versa, causing jerky operation. Much of this was based on efforts to improve emissions and fuel economy. You want high line pressure (control pressure) at WOT for firm upshifts and low line pressure during deceleration so you don't feel the downshifts with decreasing vehicle speed.
- Split-torque function causes a lot of frustration and durability issues. Although it's impossible to do away with the split-torque function, it can be improved with modifications to the valve body.
- The AOD was originally developed for light-duty applications, not high-performance V-8 engines. As a result, AODs in Mustang and LTD High Output applications struggled to stay together. As time went on, Ford engineered refinements to the AOD to improve durability.

AOD Clutch Pack Installation

1 Assemble Direct Clutch

Install the direct clutch piston seals. As with the forward clutch, some seal lips are one-direction fit only. Pay very close attention. The seal lips point toward the pressure side. (The blue grease here is transmission assembly lube.)

2 Assemble Direct Clutch Assembly

This is an AOD direct clutch iron casting with a clutch piston. The AODE/4R70W direct clutch drum is stamped steel, which reduces transmission weight and provides strength.

3 Install Direct Clutch Piston

Press the direct clutch piston into place using seal protectors to safeguard the piston seals. Seal protectors are available from most automatic transmission parts supply houses.

4 Install Direct Clutch Piston Return Spring

Use a compressor to install the direct clutch piston return spring assembly. At home, you can use four C-clamps from a hardware store. Protect your eyes and face.

Precision Measurement

5 Check Clutch Steel Thicknesses

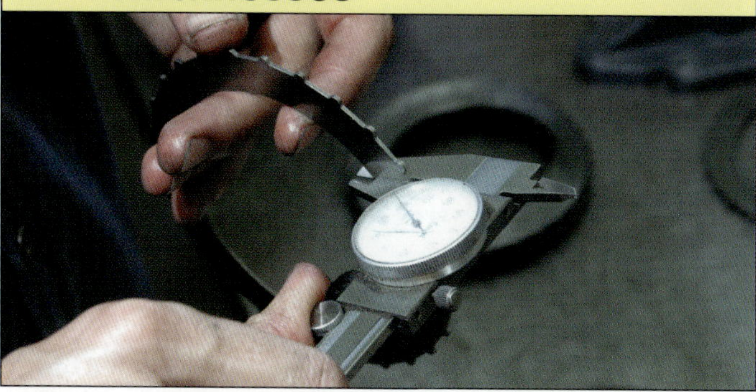

Clutch plates can be of varying thicknesses. They wear at different rates, which is why thickness can vary. Also, clutch plates don't always come from the same sources, which affects thickness. Each steel plate should be measured with calipers prior to installation. Do the same with clutch discs after you saturate them in fluid.

6 Install Direct Clutch Thrust Bearing

The direct clutch needs a thrust bearing if you're going with an original AOD geartrain. AOD transmissions with an AODE/4R70W geartrain upgrade have Torrington bearings instead of thrusts.

7 Install Direct Clutch Hub

The direct clutch needs this clutch hub, which splines into the clutch frictions. Examine the teeth for scoring and other types of damage. Make sure the clutch teeth slide smoothly in this hub.

8 Install Direct Clutch Steels and Frictions

The direct clutch discs and plates drop in alternately. Clearances are .040 to .057 inch for V-6s and .050 to .067 inch for V-8s. Measure the clearances between the pressure plate and the first disc.

You can improve clutch pack durability with a combination of larger-capacity direct and forward clutches by either performing modifications to your existing clutch drums, or by opting for the aftermarket. A trusted machine shop can cut a new groove for the snap ring that allows you to add clutch friction and steel plates.

Another solution is the E8LY-7F283-A direct clutch drum first used in the AOD in 1988, which accommodates one additional clutch disc and plate, for a total of six clutches. There is also a vast selection in the performance transmission aftermarket for Ford's AOD, where you can stuff seven and eight clutches into the direct clutch.

AOD versus AODE/4R70W Direct Clutch Comparison

The AOD direct clutch (right) is an iron machining with fewer clutch teeth. It is also heavier, with less fluid-scavenging efficiency. The AODE/4R70W direct clutch (left) is lighter because it is stamped steel. It is also stronger, with more clutch steel teeth and better fluid-scavenging efficiency via fluid-scavenging holes around the perimeter.

Do you see the difference between these two direct clutch plates? The AODE/4R70W clutch plate (left) has more teeth. The AOD clutch plate (right) with fewer teeth also has less contact area.

AODE/4R70W Clutch Pack Installation

1 Install Direct Clutch

The AODE/4R70W direct clutch assembles the same way as the AOD. The clutch piston goes in first, with seal lips pointed toward the clutch cylinder and away from the clutches and plates.

Precision Measurement

2 Use Spring Compressor or C-Clamp

You can use a spring compressor to compress the clutch piston return spring (shown). You may also use C-clamps. A C-clip holds the springs and clutch piston in place.

3 Install Thrust Bearing

The Torrington bearing is also known as the number-7 needle bearing. It has a support ring, and must be installed first.

4 Inspect and Install Direct Clutch Hub

The direct clutch hub sits in the center of the direct clutch drum. The clutch hub should be checked for irregularities that may hinder clutch friction movement.

5 Install Direct Clutch Discs and Plates

Drop the direct clutch discs and plates into the clutch cylinder. Install the snap ring and check clearances. Clearances with the AODE/4R70W direct clutch should be .060 to .091 inch between discs and plates.

6 Apply Assembly Lube

Install the direct clutch Torrington bearing and use liberal amounts of assembly lube. The direct clutch seats in the ring gear/output shaft assembly.

Building a Better AOD

While you're thinking about performance upgrades, don't forget basic improvements such as bushings, thrusts, and bearings. Hard parts are rugged and can typically survive several overhauls. However, transmissions that have been sorely neglected can wind up with hard parts that are little more than recyclable metal due to dirty fluid and extreme wear. Reusing worn hard parts can lead to premature transmission failure because the same problem will persist.

Hard parts such as the planet carrier should be closely inspected for unusual wear. Planet gears should feel solid with no wobble, indicating acceptable inside gear and bushing wear. They should also show wear and not have a mirror finish, which is typically excessive wear. Planet and sun gears need to fit one another with great precision or they wear out prematurely.

When clutch drums are disassembled, they should be closely inspected for burred and ragged clutch plate grooves that can hang up clutch discs and steel plates, causing a malfunction. Seal contact surfaces should be true and free from scoring. Rough surfaces should be dressed until smooth and serviceable. Examine clutch pistons for scoring and irregularities that can damage seals.

Replace Bushings

Replace all bushings during your AOD build, even though many transmission builders rarely do this because it is time consuming. When bushings are replaced, bathe them with plenty of transmission assembly lube for a safe start-up. Use no lubricant between the bushing and casting. You want solid bushing security. ■

Output Shaft and Direct Clutch Assembly

1 Install Output Shaft Sealing Rings

Install the number-5 and number-6 output shaft sealing rings. Color and type are important for proper installation and leakage prevention. Beige sealing rings (shown) are for the output shaft and direct clutch.

Install the number-7 through number-10 output shaft sealing rings. The ring gear has already been fitted.

2 Install Direct Clutch Assembly

The direct clutch slips inside the ring gear onto the output shaft where those beige sealing rings are. Make sure you have lubed everything for smooth assembly and function.

The direct clutch has to be twisted and finessed into the ring gear and onto the output shaft. Again, everything must have generous amounts of lubrication.

Assembling clutch packs and other subassemblies requires the detail of neurosurgery because it is so easy to make a mistake when installing seals, snap rings, and clutches. Because seals tear and distort easily, they need generous amounts of lubrication.

Some seals are designed to install in one direction only. If you're working with a clutch piston seal with a lip, the lip must be pointed toward the pressure source or inside the clutch cylinder. With the lip pointed toward the pressure source, you get a fail-safe installation because pressure holds the seal lip against the sealing surface. Installing a directional clutch piston seal backward means leakage and the absence of clutch function from pressure loss.

Regardless of the type of clutch piston seal you are working with, there must be solid contact between the seal, piston, and cylinder.

The intermediate clutches stacked in front of the case can be upgraded by using some of the AODE/4R70W intermediate clutches, which adds clutch capacity. You should use the F3LY-7B006-A clutch plate in place of the stock AOD intermediate clutch plate. This plate provides room for more intermediate clutch frictions.

Another modification is enlarging the forward clutch apply orifice in the valve body's separator plate, which improves the quality of the 4-3 downshift. You can make dramatic improvements with genuine off-the-shelf Ford parts. To get durability from the AOD, you have to go to AODE/4R70W internals, which means the entire geartrain from forward clutch to ring gear and output shaft. All of these components are available from Ford parts sources or the aftermarket.

The single greatest improvement you can make is the AODE/4R70W reverse clutch drum and overdrive band. The AOD's 1½-inch-wide overdrive band doesn't exhibit enough holding power. The AODE/4R70W's wider 2-inch band and drum makes a huge difference in durability. You should also use a Kevlar-faced 2-inch overdrive band for extreme-duty service.

Component Comparisons

The AODE and 4R70W have very distinct differences based on gearing and the reverse drum/overdrive band. If you're building an AODE and want to make it better, opt for 4R70W components, which offer durability and better gearing. ■

On the left is an AODE/4R70W planet carrier with the close-ratio 2.84:1/.70. On the right is an AOD 2.40:1/.67.

The reverse drum is held stationary by the overdrive band. It is often mistakenly called the "overdrive" drum. The one on the right is an AOD. The one on the left is an AODE/4R70. Its tabs are longer for increased strength. This drum is also wider for increased overdrive band width and holding capacity.

Here are two inverted planet carriers: the one on the left has a close-ratio 2.84:1/.70; the one on the right has a wide-ratio 2.40:1/.67. These planetaries interchange as long as you have all compatible components with them. When you perform this swap, you need the entire AODE/4R70W geartrain.

These are inverted reverse clutch drums. An AODE/4R70W is on the left and an AOD is on the right. The AODE/4R70W is wider and larger for improved clutch and band engagement. The narrow 1½-inch overdrive band has always been a weakness on the AOD. The AOD has more clutch plate teeth for improved engagement. At first, it appeared as though the clutch drum on the left had a broken tooth but it was a running production change.

Here are reverse clutch drums with overdrive bands. On the left is an AODE/4R70W with the wider band. On the right is an AOD with the 1½-inch band. The wider AODE/4R70W band and reverse drum offer greater holding power.

Component Comparisons *CONTINUED*

Ring gear assemblies from an AODE/4R70W are on the left and an AOD is on the right. Both ring gears can be used only with their related geartrain components: only AOD ring gears with AOD parts and AODE/4R70W ring gears with AODE/4R70W parts.

These inverted ring gears demonstrate the differences between an AOD and an AODE/4R70W. If you remove the snap rings, the hubs are easily removed. The AODE/4R70W ring gear and hub assembly has drain holes around the perimeter, which is the easiest way to identify it.

An AODE/4R70W sun gear is on the left and an AOD sun gear is on the right. At first glance it's difficult to see the difference. Look for the oil-scavenge hole in the AODE/4R70W sun gear.

The AODE/4R70W drive shell on the left is beveled to accommodate the larger AODE/4R70W reverse clutch. An AOD drive shell is on the right.

Reverse, Intermediate and Forward Clutch Assembly

1 Install Reverse Clutch Apply Piston

Pay close attention to the seal lip direction when you install the reverse clutch piston. The seal lip must be pointed toward the pressure source (toward the cylinder). The seals and piston should have generous lubrication to prevent scoring or distortion. Don't forget the retaining ring.

2 Install Belleville Spring

The Belleville spring is a clutch piston return spring. Belleville springs tend to split and break, which calls for close attention to detail during disassembly and assembly.

Precision Measurement

3 Install Apply Plate

Before you install the clutches and plates, install the reverse clutch apply plate. Inspect the pressure plate for scoring and warping.

4 Install Reverse Clutch Frictions and Steels

Alternate reverse clutch frictions with steel plates. Although clutch frictions aren't wet here, they should be soaked prior to installation to get the proper operating thicknesses so the clearances are right. Not all transmission techs agree with this; however, there's nothing to be lost by soaking them ahead of time. It is also a good idea to soak clutch friction discs ahead of time for accurate measurement.

5 Install Reverse Clutch Pressure Plate

Install the pressure plate and snap ring last. Check the clutch clearances; they should be .030 to .056 inch for 5.0L V-8s and 3.8L V-6s, or .040 to .075 inch for 5.8L (351-ci) V-8s. Snap rings of varying thicknesses are available to get the clearances right.

6 Install Intermediate Clutch Snap Ring

Secure the intermediate one-way clutch snap ring. Check the one-way clutch for smooth, noise-free operation. It should turn freely in one direction and lock up in the other.

7 Install Forward Clutch and Thrust Bearing

Inspect the clutch grooves and install the forward clutch and thrust bearing. Mate the reverse clutch to the forward clutch and input shaft.

8 Assemble Reverse and Forward Clutches

Stack the reverse clutch drum on top of the forward clutch and input shaft. Seat the reverse clutch drum and check the one-way clutch for freedom of operation.

If your budget allows (this is a very important upgrade), invest in the larger "A" overdrive band servo for solid engagement without slippage and heat. You should use the 4340 chrome-moly input shaft for the AOD, which is available from a number of sources and withstands 700 to 800 hp. One-piece input shafts that combine the inner and outer input shafts bypass the overdrive lockup feature entirely if efficiency isn't important and performance is everything. It keeps you on the torque converter in torque multiplication mode for crisp acceleration.

Options are available for the AOD performance enthusiast. LenTech builds some of the strongest racing automatics in the world, specializing in the AOD, AODE, and 4R70W. One of the AOD's greatest shortcomings is dual-input shafts (a shaft within a shaft) in a split-torque function. LenTech addresses this issue with a non-locking overdrive, which means the engine stays on the torque multiplication side of the converter for better acceleration even in third gear. You don't get the efficiency of a direct lockup; however, you do get improved performance.

Case Components Assembly

1 Begin Case Assembly

Install the number-9 Torrington bearing (needle bearing) assembly. Pack the bearing with plenty of transmission assembly lube. All thrust washers and bearings should be new in the interest of durability.

2 Replace Manual and Throttle Valve Shaft Seals

While the case is bare, replace the manual and throttle valve shaft seals and check the shafts for scoring and distortion. Take care to avoid seal distortion and use plenty of lube.

3 Lubricate Manual Shift and Throttle Valve Shafts

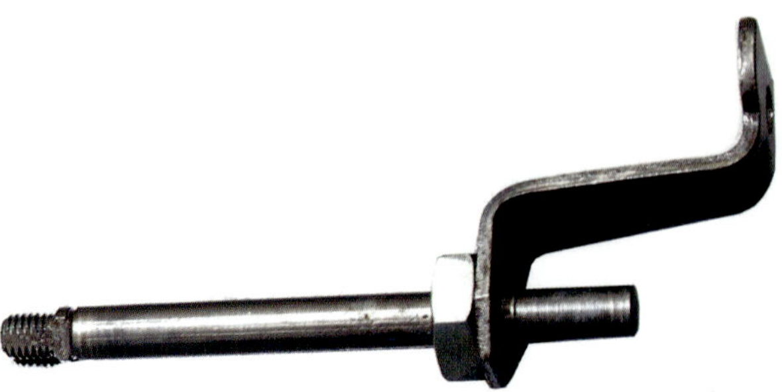

The manual shift (left) and throttle valve shaft (right) should be lubricated with transmission assembly lube, then mated and installed in the case.

4 Install Manual Shift and Throttle Valve Shafts

Install the manual and throttle valve shafts with new seals. Position the throttle valve return spring as shown. This is a very tight configuration for an open-end wrench.

5 Inspect Parking Pawl

Here's the parking pawl actuating rod and cam out of park with the pawl disengaged. The rod and cam should be lubricated with assembly lube.

6 Inspect Parking Pawl CONTINUED

This the parking pawl actuating rod and cam in park with the parking pawl engaged. The cam pushes the parking pawl into the rear gear, locking the output shaft.

From inside the case, you can see that the parking pawl engages the ring gear assembly, locking the output shaft. The parking pawl locks into the ring gear when the selector is placed in park.

LenTech goes beyond the torque converter and geartrain in its quest for performance; it also looks at hydraulics. The factory settings adversely affect performance because upshift tends to occur too early. AOD racers have long known you can upshift from first to third gear and then downshift quickly to first gear before upshifting into third. The transmission stays in second until it is necessary to shift into third.

The problem with this approach is precious lost time and undue stress on the overdrive band and drum. LenTech modifies the AOD valve body, which allows you to upshift normally, 1-2-3-4. LenTech also performs a solenoid overdrive control modification, which allows manual control.

Internal Final Assembly

1 Install Output Shaft and Ring Gear

You install the output shaft, ring gear, and direct clutch assembly as a unit. You can see the direct clutch, which receives the smaller input shaft during final assembly.

2 Install Low-Reverse Band

Position the low-reverse band in the case around the ring gear assembly and locate it on the anchor pins. Make sure it is positioned where the servo actuating rod meets the band. As with clutch discs, the low-reverse band should be lubricated with transmission fluid for installation.

3 Inspect Output Shaft Assembly

With the output shaft, ring gear assembly, direct clutch, and low-reverse band in place, it becomes clear how these components fit together in the case. The servo has not yet been installed.

4 Install Planet Carrier One-Way Clutch

The one-way clutch fits into the planet carrier. The carrier and one-way clutch should be lubed with transmission assembly lube and checked for proper operation. Check the one-way clutch rollers and cage for integrity. The one-way clutch should be replaced in the interest of durability.

5 Fit Steel Center Support

Seat the stamped-steel center support in the planet carrier and check for smooth operation against the one-way clutch. It should turn one way but not the other and do so smoothly.

6 Install Center Support

Install the center support and planet carrier. Seat them into the ring gear and direct clutch. The direct clutch can be seen here, in the middle below the planet gears.

7 Seat Direct Clutch

The planet carrier can be seated into the ring gear and direct clutch with a little twisting of the small input shaft, which is splined into the direct clutch.

8 Install Spring Tabs

The anti-clunk spring tabs must face outward to do their job properly. These springs stabilize the center support and prevent "clunking."

9 Secure Center Support

Secure the center support with a large snap ring, which has been installed. Between the snap ring and anti-clunk springs, the center support should be secure.

TECH TIP

Select Best-Quality Components

You should choose the newest-generation AOD components for your AOD build core as close to the end of AOD production as possible. Early AOD units lack the engineering revisions that occurred throughout AOD production.

The core being built in this chapter is a 1989 AOD unit with most of the AOD upgrades, meaning higher-capacity direct and forward clutches, a larger "A" overdrive servo, and additional intermediate clutches.

You also need to be aware of hydraulic control refinements with the installation of any number of shift improvement kits (see Chapter 5 for more details). ■

Intermediate Internal Assembly

1 Install Sun Gear and Thrust Bearings

Fit the sun gear into the planet gears, which can be tricky. With the sun gear comes the number-5 thrust bearing, which is located on the sun gear head. The number-5 thrust bearing goes between the sun gear and drive shell (which you install next). Coat the gear teeth and bearing with assembly lube and work the sun gear back and forth. This should seat the sun gear firmly.

2 Install Drive Shell

The drive shell fits into the planet carrier right after the sun gear and rides the number-5 thrust bearing.

3 Install Number-4 Thrust Bearing

Inside the drive shell is this number-4 thrust bearing, which buffers against the reverse clutch and one-way clutch assembly. Generous lubrication is best with each of these assemblies.

4 Fit Forward Clutch Hub into Drive Shell

This is the forward clutch hub, which is seated in the drive shell. It receives the number-3 thrust bearing (shown). The reverse and forward clutches ride against this bearing. The reverse clutch frictions spline into this hub.

5 Install Reverse and Forward Clutches

Spline the reverse and forward clutch assemblies into the drive shell and clutch hub. You will likely have to rock these assemblies back and forth to get them to seat. This is the way your AOD should look once you seat the reverse clutch.

6 Install Overdrive Band

The overdrive band installs wet with transmission fluid and seats against the anchor pin. The servo places pressure against this band, locking the reverse clutch. Some people incorrectly call this the overdrive drum. It is the reverse clutch, which houses the reverse clutches and splines into the forward clutch and input shaft.

Intermediate Clutch Installation

1 Install Intermediate Clutches

Place the intermediate clutch discs and steel plates in the case. These clutches lock the reverse clutch drum. They should also be soaked in transmission fluid prior to installation.

Alternately lay the clutches and plates until the last steel. You check the intermediate clutch clearances differently from the rest, with a depth micrometer instead of a thickness gauge (a depth micrometer can be found at nearly any tool supply house). The clutch stack depth from the leading edge of the case (where the pump seats) to the first steel should be 1.634 to 1.636 inches for all V-8s and 1.629 to 1.640 inches for all V-6s. Check this depth in two locations 180 degrees apart. Clutch steels are available in four thicknesses.

Precision Measurement

2 Check Intermediate Clutch Depth

When you get to the last intermediate steel plate, check clearances with a depth micrometer. Position the depth micrometer at the pump to the transmission face and take the measurement from there to the clutch plate.

Front Pump Assembly Installation

1 Install Front Pump Thrust Washer

The nylon thrust washer sets up clearance between the pump and reverse clutch assembly. Clearance should be .030 to 056 inch for V-6s and .040 to .075 inch for V-8s.

2 Install Pump Gasket

Lay a thin film of transmission assembly lube on the pump gasket and transmission mating surface. Make sure all passages are properly lined up. Aslo check the pump passages for proper alignment.

3 Install Front Pump

Carefully position the front pump and love-tap it into place with a mallet. Confirm the bolt-hole alignment by hand-threading bolts and carefully run the bolts down. Torque bolts in a crisscross pattern to 16 to 20 ft-lbs.

4 Install Secondary Input Shaft

Insert the secondary input shaft and splined into the direct clutch, which cannot be seen, but is felt when the shaft is seated. The secondary input shaft joins the geartrain when you are in overdrive/lockup.

Servo Upgrades

AOD factory evolution includes larger servos to increase durability. Early on, the AOD was fitted with the "C" overdrive servo, which is the smallest. Beginning in 1985, Ford enlarged the overdrive servo (known as the "B" servo), which increased apply force by 30 percent, according to Ford. The "B" servo includes the piston (PN E0AZ-7F200-B) and the cover (PN E0AZ-7D027-D). The best overdrive servo, which is being used in this application, is the "A" servo with the piston (PN E9SZ-7F200-A) and the cover (PN E9SZ-7D027-A). The "A" overdrive piston increases band holding power by nearly 50 percent and without any transmission modifications.

Band and Servo Installation

1 Align Bands for Servos

Manipulate the geartrain and bands so the servos and band actuating rods line up. The bands should be seated against the anchor pins at this point.

2 Install Low-Reverse Servo

Install the low-reverse servo, ensuring the piston and bore are liberally lubricated with transmission assembly lube. Make sure the actuating rod is firmly seated in the band.

3 Install Low-Reverse Servo Cover

Use a snap ring to install the low-reverse servo cover. Apply pressure on the cover and seat the snap ring. Because snap rings can pop out, make sure it is firmly seated.

4 Install Overdrive Band Servo

Give the overdrive band servo cover and its seals plenty of lubrication. Make sure the seals are free of distortion and sit squarely in the grooves. It is generally a good idea to wash the seals before lubricating them.

5 Install Overdrive Servo Piston

Lube the overdrive band servo piston before installation. Again, pay close attention to seal integrity. Any distortion will cause servo malfunction.

6 Install Servo Piston Return Spring

This is the 1989 level E9SP "A" overdrive servo, which offers the broadest surface area and greatest holding power.

7 Install Overdrive Piston and Cover

Note the generous lubrication used here. You can never have too much. Pay very close attention to the seals as you press the piston into the bore. They're easily distorted and damaged.

8 Seat Servo and Cover

Seat the piston and cover gingerly with a hammer handle and snap ring installed. Make sure the servo actuating rod is seated in the overdrive band.

9 Match Piston Rod and Band

This is what proper actuating rod and band installation looks like. The rod should be seated in the band as shown.

Overhaul Clearances

Turbine/Stator Endplay

Forward Clutch: .040 to .071 inch (3.8L V-6), .050 to .089 inch (V-8)

Direct Clutch: .040 to .057 inch (3.8L V-6), .050 to .067 inch (V-8)

Reverse Clutch: .030 to .056 inch (3.8L V-6), .040 to .075 inch (V-8)

Intermediate Clutch: 1.628 to 1.640 inches (3.8L V-6) 1.634 to 1.646 inches (V-8)

Thrust

Green: .050 to .054 inch

Yellow: .068 to .072 inch

Natural: .085 to .089 inch

Red: 1.535 to 1.551 inches

Blue: 1.552 to 1.568 inches

Low-Reverse Piston

.112 to .237-inch travel

Low-Reverse Piston

2.936-inch rod length with one groove

2.989-inch rod length with two grooves

3.043-inch rod length with three grooves

Pressure

Main Tap: 75 to 90 psi in reverse at idle
241 to 290 psi in reverse at WOT

Forward Clutch: 55 to 65 psi in drive at idle
176 to 215 psi in drive at WOT

Throttle Valve: 0 to 3 psi in drive at idle
70 to 91 psi in drive at WOT

Fluid Capacity

12.3 quarts (11.6 liters, 10.2 Imperial quarts) ■

Band Upgrade

Upgrade to the AOD "A" overdrive servo and get better band engagement without having to pull the transmission. All you have to do is carefully drop the valve body for servo access. The "A" servo was factory installed from 1988-up. If you have an older 1980–1987 AOD, the "A" servo upgrade is easy to accomplish and can be done with the transmission in the car.

If you cannot find the "A" servo, TCI Automotive Jumbo Servo (PN 436003) delivers greater band gripping power. And when you combine the Jumbo Servo with TCI's High Performance Overdrive Bands for AOD or AODE/4R70W reverse clutch drums (also called overdrive drums), holding power is vastly improved. The transmission must be removed from the vehicle and disassembled to perform a band upgrade. ■

Control Improvements

The throttle valve does the work of two components: the vacuum modulator and the kickdown linkage. The vacuum modulator in earlier Ford automatics regulates control pressure based on load and throttle position.

The throttle valve's function is quite simple. Based on throttle position and cable/rod tension, the throttle valve handles control pressure to all servos and clutches. When you go to wide-open throttle (WOT), you want high-control pressure for a firm upshift. The firm upshift comes from solid clutch and band engagement.

TV Cable Adjustment

Use a pressure gauge for TV cable/rod adjustment, but also observe transmission function. Don't go by throttle valve pressure alone. Indicated pressure doesn't always mean adjustment is where you'd like it. You want a firm upshift timed with the way you are driving.

At WOT, there should be a hard upshift at high RPM. If there is slippage and upshift is early, cable tension isn't high enough.

During normal acceleration, you should have a predictable 1-2-3-4 upshift. Upshifts that occur too early not only hinder acceleration, they burn clutches and bands because line pressure isn't high enough for firm engagement. Make your adjustments in minute steps between test drives.

Be very careful with your test drives. Push it hard and you can ruin a fresh transmission. Conduct your test drives with mild to moderate acceleration at first, make adjustments, and continue test driving. ■

If there isn't enough line pressure, clutches and bands slip, generating excessive heat and friction material loss.

By the same token, low cable/rod tension softens the upshift because line pressure is lower and slippage is more apparent. What you want from the TV cable or rod adjustment is a later, firmer upshift without being too firm. Ford strongly suggests using a line pressure gauge for TV cable or rod adjustment. This is an adjustment that must be precise or it can cause serious transmission damage.

AOD applications fitted with central fuel injection or a carburetor employ a throttle valve rod instead of a cable, which calls for a different type of adjustment on a spring-loaded control rod and pivot at the transmission. There's also an adjustment at the throttle body or carburetor. In applications with TV cables, adjustment is at one location at the throttle body. Cable tension is controlled at the throttle body (see Chapter 9).

Regardless of whether you have a TV cable or rod, adjustment boils down to how and when the transmission shifts during normal driving and WOT. During normal acceleration, you want a firm (but not hard) shift. At WOT you want a hard upshift when the engine reaches its torque peak for best results. During deceleration, downshifting automatically is normal and you should never feel it. If you can, control pressure is too high. Line pressure should be low at light or no throttle and high at WOT.

Aftermarket service and valve body kits for the AOD contribute to improved shift quality and transmission life. These kits are available separately and they're also included in overhaul kits. TCI Automotive transmission overhaul kits, for example, include just about everything you need to rebuild an AOD, including all soft parts such as gaskets and seals, friction discs and steel clutches, low-reverse and overdrive bands, filter, and servo pistons. And when you build, you want to choose a torque converter from one of many manufacturers such as B&M, LenTech, TCI Automotive, TransGo, Bowler, and others, based on how you intend to use your AOD.

Accumulator and Valve Body Installation

1 Install 2-3 Accumulator Piston

Lube the 2-3 shift accumulator piston and seat it in the bore. This installation varies from generation to generation as there were running production changes. The 2-3 shift accumulator was finally perfected by the 1989 model year and is available from a variety of transmission parts suppliers.

2 Install Accumulator Return Spring

Next, install the 2-3 shift accumulator return springs. Some applications have two springs; others have one. The best example to go by is the transmission you have and the model year unit you're working with.

3 Lay Down Valve Body Gasket

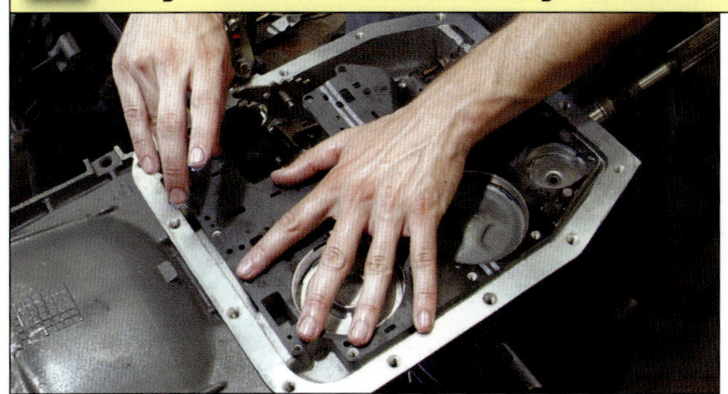

Place the valve body gasket. Make sure all surfaces are hospital clean. Even the smallest speck of dust can cause leakage and pressure loss. You can use a thin film of transmission assembly lube for gasket security.

4 Install Valve Body

This valve body has been rebuilt and fitted with a TCI Automotive shift kit for firm shifts and less wear and tear. Valve body installation mandates the utmost care with proper bolt placement.

5 Check Manual and Throttle Valve Alignment

The manual and throttle valves should be checked for proper operation. The manual valve has detents to keep it in the selected gear range. The throttle valve is linear and spring loaded. Make sure both valves operate smoothly without sticking.

Do an operation check of these valves using compressed air.

Torque Fasteners

6 Torque Valve Body Bolts

Torque the valve body bolts to 80 to 100 in-lbs beginning with light hand tightening to seat the valve body, then torquing in one-third increments.

Governor Installation

1 Air Check Servos and Clutches

Check the servos and clutches with air via the output shaft's governor passages. When air is applied, listen for servo and clutch piston movement.

2 Rebuild Governor

Disassemble, clean, and inspect the governor, which is mounted on the output shaft. From left to right are the end plug, sleeve, spring, governor valve, governor main body, cover with two bolts, and counterweight attachment screws. (Not shown here is the counterweight.) A small filtering screen should always be included. Some transmissions are missing this screen due to previous rebuilds. The screen can be cleaned or replaced. Most transmission parts supply houses have them.

Critical Inspection

3 Inspect Governor

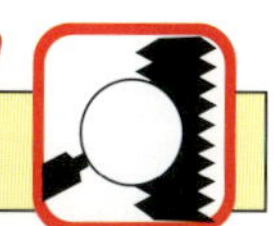

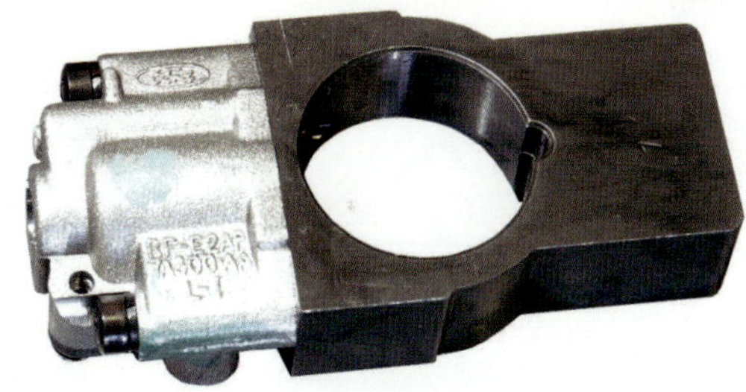

The governor spins on the output shaft, affecting line pressure as vehicle speed changes. Shake the governor back and forth to ascertain valve freedom and movement.

4 Install Governor Assembly

The governor slides onto the output shaft. The ball acts as a drive key, much like a square key in a keyway. If the ball is missing, the governor does not function properly.

5 Secure Governor with Snap Ring

The snap ring keeps the governor in place on the output shaft. Make sure the snap ring is deeply seated and secure.

6 Install Tailshaft Housing Gasket

Install the tailshaft housing gasket using a thin film of assembly lube for adhesion and sealing. The tailshaft housing is also known as the extension housing.

7 Tighten Housing Bolts

Install and secure the extension housing. The bolts should be torqued to 16 to 20 ft-lbs in a crisscross fashion.

8 Choose Pan and Gasket

The transmission pan goes on next, using the best gasket available. Use a composite silicone/steel combination originally used by Ford, which seals like no other gasket.

9 Install Pan

Torque the bolts to 6 to 10 ft-lbs. Avoid using a cork or cork/rubber gasket because they leak.

The automotive performance transmission aftermarket enjoys a wealth of options for building an AOD or AODE/4R70W. Most AOD performance parts are little more than off-the-shelf Ford pieces that were factory upgrades made over the production life of both the AOD and AODE/4R70W transmissions. The entire AODE/4R70W geartrain can be swapped into the AOD with great results, which takes the confusion out of improving the AOD. Dynax frictions, which have a proven track record are a great choice for an AOD build. As mentioned previously, the wider 2-inch overdrive band and reverse clutch drum improve durability. The wide-ratio 4R70W gearset improves acceleration with a 2.84:1 first gear winding out to a .70 overdrive ratio. If you have the budget, the aftermarket has your 4R70W performance parts.

Baumann Electronic Controls offers a wide variety of performance parts and control systems for the AOD. The ReCalPro Valve Body Recalibration Kit raises full-throttle shift-points about 1,100 rpm. It is all about fine-tuning the pressure control system where you get both performance and durability.

Once you get the hydraulic control system where it needs to be for improved performance and durability, you want solid mechanicals to back it up. One AOD weakness is the direct clutch. It can be remedied by the Alto Direct Clutch Pack Kit, which allows you to increase the number of clutches to seven or eight. You have a choice of the AOD's cast-iron direct clutch drum or the stamped steel, which is lighter.

The Sonnax Pressure Regulator Boost Valve, available from a variety of aftermarket transmission performance suppliers, is another path to performance and durability because it solves pressure regulation issues that have long plagued the AOD. This kit consists of the booster valve and a sleeve that eliminates the sticking pressure regulator boost valve problem and resulting failure.

You should stay with a stock Ford transmission pan because they are of the best quality. They also fit best and don't leak. Another solution is a Ford Bronco AOD pan, which is deeper and has greater capacity. If you want more fluid capacity and better cooling, go with a finned cast-aluminum pan. This type gets rid of heat best, thanks to its cooling fins and the heat transfer advantages of cast aluminum.

Keep a close eye on casting porosity with cast aluminum, which can cause leakage. Casting porosity is a fundamental weakness in aluminum and iron castings where excessive amounts of air get into the molten mixture before it cools and cures. The casting becomes more like a sponge, allowing fluid to leak through the casting and onto your garage floor. You can coat the inside of the cast pan with GE Glyptal, which is an excellent sealer. The key to success with Glyptal is good paint adhesion, which means you must have a clean surface before application. If the pan already had transmission fluid in it, do not use Glyptal.

As you assemble your AOD transmission, be aware of torque specifications and follow them to the letter. Incorrect torque can do permanent damage, especially to lightweight aluminum castings that depend on precise tension and bolt stretch. When you are assembling clutch packs, check clutch plate clearances and follow specifications to the letter. During final assembly, always check endplay.

Torque Specifications

Component	*Foot-Pounds*
Front Pump to Case	16 to 20
Stator to Pump	16 to 25
Oil Pan	6 to 10
Extension Housing	16 to 20
Throttle Valve Shaft	19 to 27
Manual Shift Shaft	12 to 16
Bellhousing	40 to 50
Backup Light/Neutral Safety Switch	8 to 11
Torque Converter Plug	8 to 28
Pressure Port Plugs	6 to 12
Torque Converter/Flexplate	20 to 34
Torque Converter Dust Cover	12 to 16
Push Connect Fitting	18 to 23

Component	*Inch-Pounds*
Detent Spring Bolt	80 to 120
Valve Body Reinforcement Plate	80 to 120
Separator Plate	80 to 120
Governor to Counterweight	80 to 120
Governor Cover	34 to 50
Valve Body	80 to 120
Filter Bolts	80 to 120 ■

AOD Shift Kits

Although it is widely believed shift improvement kits are for improving performance, they are also about improving durability. A soft upshift, particularly at WOT, is caused by clutch and band slippage, which generates heat and puts excessive friction material in the fluid. Friction material and metal particulates damage seals and moving parts. As seals wear, line pressure deteriorates, causing more slippage and heat. Heat tends to cook the fluid, doing further damage.

For the street, you want a firm upshift without heat and slippage that doesn't jar your teeth out. A firm, seamless upshift indicates quick, solid band and clutch engagement. There are many shift improvement kits in the marketplace, including those that come with overhaul kits custom tailored to the kind of driving you intend to do.

Because Tom's Transmissions used a TCI Automotive transmission overhaul kit in Chapter 4, it was decided to use TCI Automotive's Trans-Scat kit for the 1980–1993 Ford AOD (PN 436000).

TCI Automotive offers three Trans-Scat kits for the AOD: Street, Street/Strip, and Heavy Duty. These are commonsense shift improvement kits designed to improve line pressure and control, thereby improving shifts with solid clutch and band engagement.

Even the most seasoned transmission tech needs to closely follow the shift improvement kit instructions. No two manufacturers have the same approach to shift improvement kits. Never mix parts from different kits, and always follow instructions.

Compatibility

Never mix transmission shift improvement kits and parts from different manufacturers. Each manufacturer has a different approach to shift improvement kits. When you mix parts, it can cause a malfunction and transmission damage. Stick with one type of shift kit from one manufacturer and play it safe. ■

Tom's Transmissions is working with two AOD valve bodies. One has been modified (shown) just to show you a modified valve body. The other core (not shown), is the build candidate. The AOD valve bodies vary considerably between 1980 and 1993. Closely examine the casting numbers to determine what core you have.

TCI's Trans-Scat shift improvement kit (PN 436000) is available in three forms: Street, Street/Strip, and Heavy Duty. For your street and weekend racing application, consider the Street/Strip kit. You want Heavy Duty for police, taxi, and towing, which delivers a firm, but not aggressive, shift.

The street version delivers a firmer upshift than stock, improving durability.

They build the street/Strip Trans-Scat into every Street Fighter transmission for tire-barking firm upshifts. This means no slippage, better transmission of power, and increased durability.

The heavy-duty version is for severe-duty use in police, taxi, and towing applications where you get a firm, but not harsh, shift.

This kit can be installed on a workbench, where everything is easy to see and understand, rather than on a lift. As the valve body is disassembled, note where parts go via the use of a good digital camera to capture the valve body as it is prior to disassembly. Be sure you capture even the smallest detail as each segment is disassembled.

The valve body should be completely disassembled with every part laid out on a clean surface in the order they came out of the valve body. Once completely disassembled, the valve body and each component should be cleaned in a solvent with a high evaporative rate or hot solvent washer to remove any sludge or debris. Then valve parts, including seals, should be soaked in automatic transmission fluid and reassembled.

Some transmission technicians suggest washing the valve body before valve parts are removed to minimize the risk of faulty reassembly, although a completely disassembled valve body with all parts removed is easier to clean internally.

Dropping a transmission pan and examining the fluid is a good way to learn about the transmission fluid condition, which immediately determines transmission health. Transmission fluid should be red/pink and clean. If it is brown or black, it is burned and the transmission should be left alone until a rebuild can be performed.

Take pictures of the valve body before it is removed. Observe the

Valve Body Disassembly

1 Disassemble Valve Body

The valve body is disassembled and carefully laid out on a clean workbench. It is a good idea to take pictures as you go to ensure parts go in the way they came out. TCI provides detailed instructions with the kit (PN 436000). Take careful notes of where fasteners, balls, and valve parts go.

Documentation Required

2 Note Check Ball Locations

This disassembled AOD valve body clearly demonstrates where the check balls go (arrows). When you remove the valve body's separator plate, be careful not to spill the ball check valves before shooting an image of where they go.

3 Remove Valves

Brian Fortune of Tom's Transmissions removes each check valve, taking note of location. Even savvy transmission builders must take note of where the check balls go because there are endless variations.

4 Wash Valve Body in Solvent

The valve body is washed with an environmentally friendly solvent and then a high-evaporative solvent to dry it out. A high-evaporative solvent, such as brake cleaner or lacquer thinner, removes all debris and moisture for reassembly.

TECH TIP

Identify Your Core

Before you disassemble the valve body, take detailed photos during each phase of disassembly, placing all parts in proper order next to the valve body. Make sure a shift kit hasn't already been installed in your AOD's valve body: this can be determined by spring type and color, and valve/parts layout. Because valve body configuration varies from generation to generation and vehicle application, there are a variety of differences. You must first ascertain what core you have and whether it has ever been apart. ■

TCI Automotive Trans-Scat Kit

TCI Automotive suggests installation in a healthy transmission. A transmission with burned fluid and damaged clutches and bands is a bad risk for a shift kit of any kind. Here is a list of components in this Trans-Scat kit:

Quantity	*Component*
3	Valve Body Gaskets
1	Filter
1	Duraprene Pan Gasket
1	Purple Throttle Valvespring
1	White Pressure Regulator Spring
1	Filter
1	Blocker Rod
1	Accumulator Spacer
1	Bolt (4 mm)
3	Drill Bits (3/32, 5/64, and 7/64 inch) ■

TCI Automotive Trans-Scat Drill Points and Sizes

Point	*Street (inch)*	*Street/Strip (inch)*	*Heavy Duty (inch)*
A	5/64	3/32	3/32
B	5/64	5/64	5/64
C	5/64	5/64	5/64
D	N/A	3/32	5/64
E	1/8	1/8	1/8
F	5/64	7/64	3/32
G	3/32	3/32	3/32
H	3/32	3/32	3/32

positioning of the manual and throttle valves. When it is time to split the valve body and separator plate, make sure the valve body is flat on the bench with the plate facing up. You don't want to lose any of the balls, check valves, or hardware.

When modifying the separator plate, refer to step 4 on page 79. That illustration also demonstrates how to modify the valve body passages where necessary. Note that orifice "H" in that illustration is a new hole/passage that is not found in your existing separator plate. Gaskets must also be modified where new holes are drilled. Keep in mind not all AOD transmissions are per that illustration, which requires close attention to detail. Very time consuming, but necessary.

When you've completed your shift enhancement kit installation, road test it to establish proper operation. While you're at it, check the line pressure with a pressure gauge. Upshifts should be firm, but not violent. If they are too firm, reduce the TV cable tension in small increments. If there's a lot of slippage and a soft shift, you don't have enough line pressure, and there's a great risk of transmission damage.

Modulator Valve Installation

1 Inspect 1-2 Accumulator Valve and 1-2 Capacity Modulator Valve

These two valve assemblies are on the driver's side: the 1-2 accumulator valve (A) and the 1-2 capacity modulator valve (B). Both require modification with parts from the Trans-Scat kit.

2 Remove 1-2 Capacity Modulator Valve

Remove the 1-2 capacity modulator valve retaining clip. The valve assembly should pop out. Pay close attention to how this valve and spring go together. Early AODs call for the use of an awl to remove the end plug.

3 Inspect Capacity Modulator Valve Layout

This is the 1-2 capacity modulator valve as installed by Ford, which is a spring and valve piston with an O-ring seal. These parts pop out for easy modification.

4 Inspect Street/Strip Configuration

If you're using the TCI Street/Strip kit, this is the configuration you want with the 1-2 capacity modulator valve. Cap over the spring (shown) following TCI's detailed instructions closely.

5 Install Street/Strip 1-2 Capacity Modulator Valve

Once you have the correct configuration, install the 1-2 capacity modulator valve. Note the cap is over the spring. For the Heavy Duty kit, flip the cap so that it isn't over the spring. This increases the spring tension. Insert the valve piston and install the clip.

Boost Regulator Valve Installation

1 Remove Main Regulator and Pressure Boost Valves

When you remove the main regulator/pressure boost valves be sure to lay them out as installed. This is the boost valve and sleeve. The valve is inside the sleeve.

2 Remove Main Pressure Regulator Valve

This is the main pressure regulator valve, which is tied to the small spring. The large white boost valvespring (inside the valve body) rests against the large washer located on the valve piston.

3 Inspect Main Regulator Pressure and Boost Valvesprings

These are the main regulator pressure spring (small) and boost valvespring (large). With the TCI kit, replace the large boost valvespring with a like spring from the kit.

4 Install TCI Boost Valvespring

Replace the large white boost valvespring with this TCI spring.

5 Reinstall Boost Valve Assembly

With the TCI spring in place, reinstall the main regulator pressure valve, springs, and boost valve. Dip the valve piston in transmission fluid for installation and ease of movement once installed.

6 Install Boost Valve/Main Pressure Regulator Valve Clip

Install this clip next. Check the valves for freedom of movement. You want to verify the proper valve function (movement) before continuing.

Throttle Valve Installation

1 Remove Throttle Valve Clip

Carefully remove the throttle valve retainer clip, making sure the valve parts are accounted for and laid out. Removal of this clip frees the throttle valve.

Documentation Required

2 Remove Throttle Valve

Remove the throttle valve assembly and lay it out in proper order. Take note of the throttle valve and all of its related pieces for easy reassembly later.

3 Install Throttle Valve Assembly

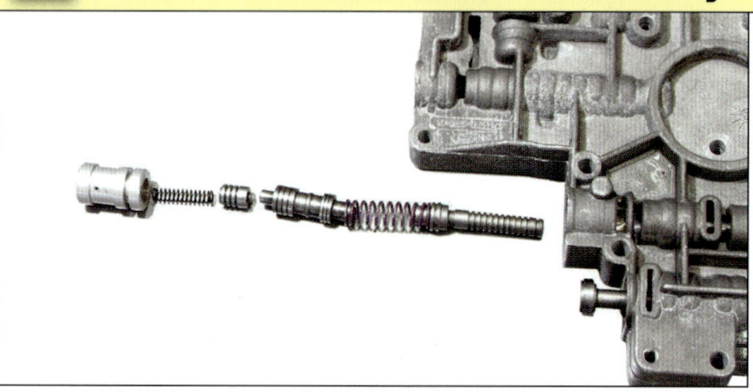

This is the throttle valve system as installed in the valve body. From left to right are the throttle sleeve, preload spring, throttle plug, throttle control valve and spring (purple), and the throttle plunger. Replace the throttle control valve spring with the purple TCI spring.

This is the throttle valve assembly completely reinstalled. The throttle valve is spring-loaded against the TV cable or rod, enabling it to return to rest when your foot is off the gas.

Passage Drilling

1 Make Room for Pin

This passage is drilled with a 7/32-inch bit to make way for the aluminum plug. Use tape on the drill bit as a guide to avoid drilling too far. Drill no farther than the bottom of the passage. The valve body must be thoroughly washed to remove any debris.

2 Install Aluminum Blockage Pin

Seal the passageway with the aluminum pin provided in the kit. It is a good idea to machine the pin before installation to keep debris out of the valve body. You want the pin flush with the valve body surface.

Professional Mechanic Tip

3 Ascertain Drill Size

PRO TIP *Mic each of the drill bits, which are included in the TCI kit, to ascertain size before you do any drilling.*

4 Choose Passages to be Drilled

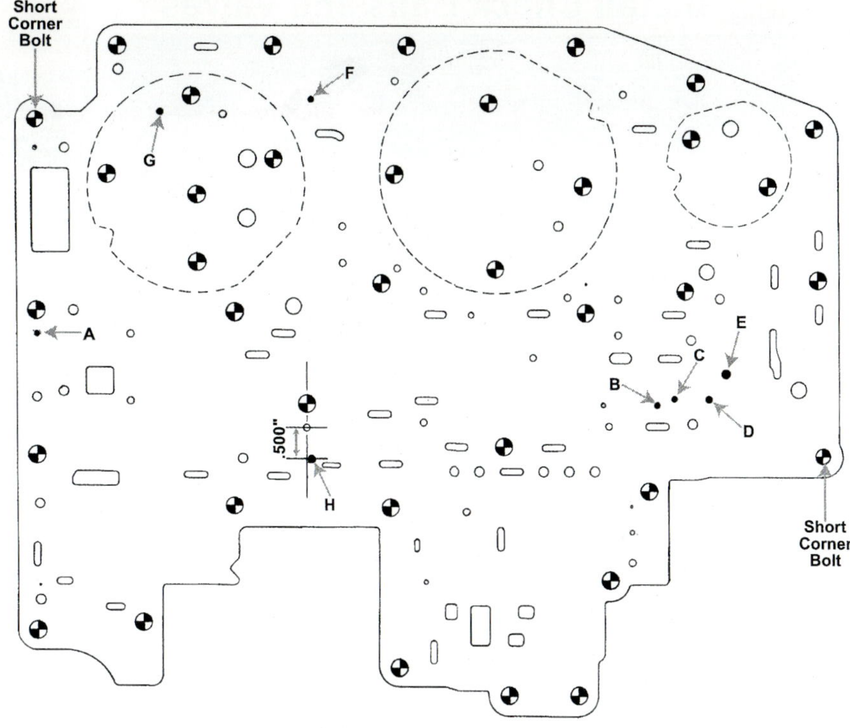

This illustration shows where modifications need to be made and in what size. Keep in mind, if you drill out the wrong hole or go too large, you will just have scrap metal and have to replace the separator plate. (Illustration Courtesy TCI Automotive)

5 Drill "A" Passage

Drill the "A" passage to 3/32 inch for the Street/Strip and Heavy Duty kits and 5/64 inch for the Street kit. Slowly and cleanly drill this passage, using transmission fluid as a lubricant. Gently deburr the hole's ragged edges with a larger bit, then wash the plate in solvent.

6 Drill "D" Passage

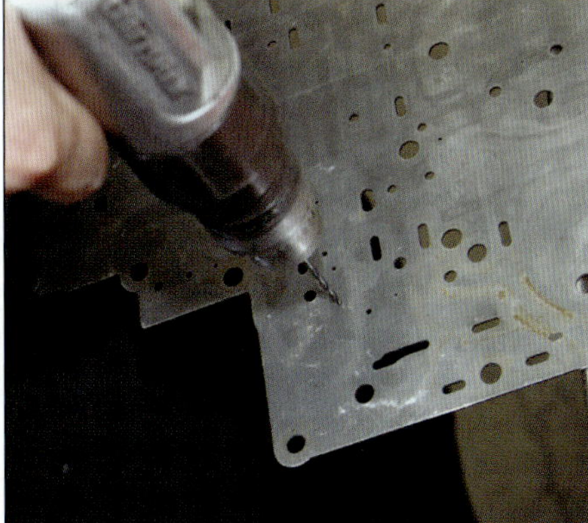

This is the "D" hole; drill it to 3/32 inch for the Street/Strip kit, 5/64 inch for the Heavy Duty kit, and not at all for the Street kit. As with the "A" passage, use a lubricant and deburr the hole.

7 Drill "F" Passage

This is the "F" hole; drill it to 7/64 inch for the Street/Strip kit, 3/32 inch for the Heavy Duty kit, and 5/64 inch for the Street kit. Deburr the passage.

Check Valve and Separator Plate Installation

1 Install Check Balls and Valves

The check ball and valve installation calls for close attention to detail, one valve at a time. TCI's instructions are very specific and easy to read, making this task straightforward. The check balls reinstall in the same locations.

Critical Inspection

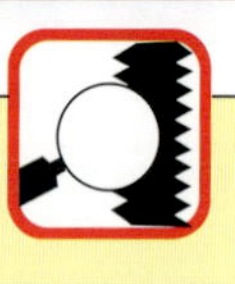

2 Inspect Check Valve Installation

There are a total of eight check balls and two linear spring-loaded valves. The two spring-loaded valves on the far left are pressure relief valves. The top one is the throttle valve pressure relief valve. The closer valve is the torque converter pressure relief valve with a blue spring. They are not interchangeable.

3 Install Valve Separator Plate and Gaskets

Be absolutely certain the valve body surfaces are hospital clean and all modified holes are clean and free of burrs and debris. Two types of gaskets are used; do not get them mixed up. The the double white–stripe gasket is for 1980–1989 and the red-stripe gasket (shown) is for 1990–1993.

4 Position and Check Separator Plate

Install the separator plate with the red-stripe 1990–1993 gasket. Check all holes/passages for accuracy and alignment. Take care not to lose any of the check balls.

5 Locate and Install Reinforcement Plates

Position the separator plate and reinforcement plates with the bolts installed. The short bolts go in the corners (see step 4 on page 79).

Torque Fasteners

6 Torque Separator and Reinforcement Plates

Torque the 11 valve body bolts crisscross evenly to 80–120 in-lbs. Be very gentle when torquing these bolts in one-third increments. See step 4 on page 79 for proper bolt placement before tightening them.

AODE/4R70W

Ford's AOD evolved into a highly successful mechanically modulated transmission from its 1980 introduction until production ended in 1991. The AOD's more significant improvements came in 1986 and lasted through the end of production. Ford developed the AODE and 4R70W to achieve cohesive engine and transmission function in 1991.

Differences from AOD

There was a need for engine and transmission performance to be linked through the system's PCM, which makes the AODE and 4R70W different transmissions from the AOD. Although these transmissions have a great deal in common, they are also very different, with limits in interchangeability. The only interchangeable components are geartrain related.

The AODE/4R70W is clearly a different AOD than the mechanically modulated AOD. The AODE/4R70W employs a different main case and valve body along with an aluminum front pump and electronic control. The driver's side has the manual shift linkage.

The AODE/4R70W is a 4-speed, rear-drive automatic overdrive with electronic control, hence the AODE designation. Ford went to electronic control not only for engine/transmission cohesion, but also improved shift quality by removing the shortcomings of mechanical control. Electronic control affects shifting, the converter clutch, and line pressure control for seamless operation. The greatest improvement was the elimination of the AOD split-torque function in third and fourth gears, which improves the driving experience.

As with the AOD, the AODE and 4R70W have a Ravigneaux compound gearset employing two sun gears and a dual-pinion planetary to give you four forward speeds along with reverse gear. There are two bands, two one-way clutches, and four friction clutches used to lock and drive the gearsets. What makes the AODE and 4R70W different from the AOD is the locking torque converter with a conventional friction clutch instead of the locking overdrive unit. The AODE/4R70W rotating mass is similar to that of the AOD. The AODE/4R70W

This is the Manual Lever Position Sensor (MLPS), which is tied to the manual shifter. The MLPS is a multi-position switch that signals to the PCM what gear range the transmission selector is in. The bolt torque is 62 to 88 in-lbs.

front pump is high-efficiency aluminum rather than iron.

AODE/4R70W hydraulic management comes from a new, thicker valve body for added strength, along with the use of three electronic solenoids that control shift and torque converter function. Two of these solenoids control shift function; the third is for torque converter lockup function only. Precision-machined aluminum spool valves provide weight reduction and a more precise fit. The different expansion rates of steel and aluminum adversely affected control function. When

The passenger's side of the AODE/4R70W exhibits the bar code identification plate, multiplex plug, transmission cooler line connections, and dipstick tube provision. The case size is the same as the AOD. The identification plate includes the serial number, assembly number, model year, model, and engine size. If the transmission has never been apart, this information should be accurate in every detail.

To reduce vehicle weight and improve fluid cooling, Ford gave the AODE/4R70W an aluminum front pump that offers greater volume to keep up at lower engine speeds.

The AODE/4R70W differs from the AOD in input. The AOD has dual input shafts (inner and outer); the AODE/4R70W has one, which splines into the forward clutch.

Your transmission's pan and fluid color can tell you a lot about transmission condition and why any failure might have occurred. Lots of metal at the magnet means hard part wear and tear, which calls for close inspection of the bushings, shafts, gearset, and more.

both spool valve and valve body expand more uniformly, function tends to be more predictable. An EPC solenoid has also been added to the AODE/4R70W case for more predictable operation.

To better tie the engine, vehicle, and transmission functions together, Ford went to an output shaft speed sensor and manual shift lever sensor, along with a multiplex electrical connector to simplify service. As the 4R70W evolved to the 4R75W, an input shaft sensor was added.

Calibration Options

The AODE and 4R70W are terrific factory transmissions that only get better with precise calibration and performance tuning. For example, the Baumann ReCalPro Valve

This is the manual shift control and detent cam. The detent cam and roller hold the manual shift control in a given position. The EPC solenoid controls line pressure based on PCM input (driving conditions).

Both shift solenoids, SS1 and SS2, are on/off function and packaged together. Adjacent is the converter clutch solenoid, which receives a pulse input for smooth engagement.

This TCI Automotive transmission overhaul kit has just about everything needed to complete an AODE/4R70W rebuild. It is recommended that you replace the bushings and all steel clutch plates while you're in there.

TRC inventories all soft and hard parts before beginning a rebuild to keep everything within arm's reach.

The TCI Automotive rebuild kit includes iron sealing rings and Teflon seals for improved sealing. Be sure you know the proper location for these sealing rings and seals.

Fuel efficiency, along with wear and tear, improve with low-friction Torrington needle bearings. When you build, use new Torringtons if possible.

Body Recalibration Kit works very well for shift improvement and durability, resulting from increased line pressure that ensures firm clutch and band engagement without destructive slippage. Further enhancements come from the Baumannator Electronic Transmission Control System, which enables you to fine-tune shift performance.

Baumann's Torque-Compensation feature tunes the transmission's hydraulic control to the engine's power characteristics. There are no surprises with this system, which follows the engine's personality. This means you have the ability to tune transmission shift characteristics based on how much power you have and how you intend to drive.

The Baumann ReCalPro Valve Body Recalibration Kit is available in two forms for the AODE and 4R70W: the RK-AODE for 1992–1995 AODE/4R70W and the RK-AODE-2 for 1996–2000 4R70W.

AODE units through 1995 are standard ratio with 2.40:1/1.47:1 gearsets, except those installed behind the 4.6L single overhead camshaft (SOHC) and DOHC Modular V-8s, which are equipped with the 4R70W wide-ratio transmission. A good rule to remember is that AODEs are standard ratio with 2.40:1/1.47:1 gearsets, while the AOD and 4R70W are wide ratio with 2.84:1/1.55:1 gearsets. The 4.6L V-8 needs the 2.84:1 and 1.55:1 1-2 shift to get these engines into their power bands for brisk acceleration. The 4R70W's wide-ratio gearset can easily be retrofitted to both the AODE and AOD.

Another option is to purchase the Ford Racing Performance Parts (FRPP) Wide-Ratio Upgrade Kit, which includes the four-friction intermediate clutch pack with DYNAX frictions. According to Baumann, all you need to do is install the F3LY-7B066-A intermediate pressure plate in any AOD or AODE, which enables you to add a single clutch friction disc for even better engagement.

The AOD full-throttle shift-point with the Motorsport wide-ratio gearset is different. Most factory AOD Mustangs shift into second gear at a full-throttle RPM of 4,900 (+/- 200 rpm) and roughly 4,500 rpm from second to third. A switch to the wide-ratio gearset increases the 1-2 shift-point by 18.3 percent (multiply 4,800 rpm by 1.183 to obtain a new shift-point of about 5,680 rpm). The 2-3 shift-point is also raised by a factor of 5.4 percent to produce a full-throttle 2-3 shift at about 4,750 rpm.

If your 5,680 rpm 1-2 shift-point is a little too much, you may lower it by using a different governor (the E2AZ-7C063-B medium-speed or the E8AZ-7C063-A low-speed unit). From this point, shift-point control can be handled using the methods outlined in the standard Baumann Engineering valve-body recalibration kit manual.

Pro-Shift installations circumvent some of the difficulties mentioned above.

Structure and Function

Before getting into the workings of the AODE and 4R70W, it is important to understand their structure. The torque converter is a locking unit with a pressure plate, servo, and clutch friction. With the locking converter comes a wider bellhousing than the AOD has. Converter function segues into a redesigned gerotor front pump with the same capacity, yet higher fluid flow in a lightweight aluminum design. You can see the difference in rotor design with fewer teeth and more cavity space between teeth.

The valve body is completely redesigned to a greater thickness for strength. Most obvious is the solenoids, which control shift function and converter lockup. To put the

Mechanical versus Electronic Malfunction

Know your AODE/4R70W's electronics. Malfunction isn't always a mechanical issue, but is oftentimes an electronics problem. Make sure all shift solenoids are functioning properly. The AODE/4R70W-series transmissions operate based on input from sensors and switches tied to the EEC-IV or EEC-V processor known as the PCM. A malfunction can exist in the PCM, which may yield a fault code but only with a Check Engine light. An electronic malfunction doesn't always provide a fault code, which means you must look to basic troubleshooting skills to find the problem.

The PCM works off signals from sensors and switches to control shift function, torque converter operation, and line pressure. Total PCM function and proper sensor/switch operation makes it all work together. Don't immediately assume there's a mechanical problem when a malfunction occurs. First, check the electronics with the proper diagnostics equipment to search for a fault code. Check the connections for corrosion and other irregularities. Check the wiring for chaffing and shorts to ground. ■

AODE/4R70W into gear, your foot must be on the brake pedal, which makes it mechanically possible to slip the selector into gear.

Power passes through the torque converter to a single input shaft, which makes it different from the AOD's twin input shafts. In final drive, however, power passes through the unit differently. Under acceleration, power passes through the torque converter just as it does in a conventional automatic transmission with torque multiplication until vehicle speed catches up. Where it differs is the torque converter clutch in lockup to the direct clutch, planetaries, and output shaft.

The torque converter shell, which is connected to the engine's crankshaft via a flexplate, drives the transmission's front pump to provide hydraulic pressure and lubrication. The torque converter's turbine drives the input shaft. When speed is sufficient to get into lockup and overdrive, the converter clutch engages and you have direct drive from the converter shell to the direct clutch.

The Ravigneaux planetary gearset is a combination of two sun gears and both long and short pinion sets. One planetary member is driven while the other is held. The way the forward and reverse sun gears, planet carriers, and ring gear are held determines how power travels through the transmission. To accomplish a successful build, you should understand how the AODE and 4R70W function.

Direct Clutch Assembly

1 Install Direct Clutch Piston Seals

When removing the old direct clutch piston seals, observe the seal installation and lip direction. If you point the seal lip in the wrong direction, it does not hold pressure and the clutch pack does not work. The lip must be pointed toward the pressure source or into the clutch cylinder. Be very careful not to scratch the clutch piston.

2 Install Direct Clutch Piston

Special Tool

Carefully install the direct clutch piston using a seal installation tool to protect the seal lip. Slowly walk the tool around, protecting the seal lip. Use an abundance of transmission assembly lube.

3 Install Direct Clutch Piston Return Springs

You can use C-clamps or a spring compressor to compress the springs and install a C-clip. Protect your eyes and face for this step.

4 Install Torrington Needle Bearing

Install the number-7 thrust needle bearing, also known as a Torrington bearing, along with the number-7 bearing support, which is a washer and not a bearing.

5 Install Number-7 C-Clip

Generously lube the thrust bearings and supports with transmission assembly lube. Install the number-7 C-clip.

6 Assemble Direct Clutch Pack

This is the direct clutch, steels, and thrust/needle bearings. All that is needed now are clutch discs between the clutch plates. Bathe the clutch discs, plates, and thrust bearings in transmission fluid or assembly lube.

7 Install Direct Clutch Hub

The direct clutch hub goes up against the number-7 thrust bearing. Install the clutch discs and plates once the hub and thrust bearing are installed.

8 Install Direct Clutch Discs and Plates

Install the direct clutch discs and plates alternately. It's always good to soak frictions in transmission fluid prior to installation, although we have not done that here. Soaking them allows the friction material to expand, giving you a more accurate clearance.

9 Install Direct Clutch Snap Ring

With all clutches and steels installed and clearances checked (.060–.091 inch), install the snap ring. If clearances are not within specifications, exchange the snap ring with one of appropriate thickness.

10 Install Direct Clutch Needle Bearing

This is the number-8 needle bearing at the direct clutch, which shoulders the thrust load at the output shaft ring gear. It is recommended that you lube the thrust bearing with transmission assembly lube for a good wet start-up.

11 Install Output Shaft Sealing Rings

Four iron sealing rings install on the output shaft. There are four grooves but just three sealing rings. The sealing rings (PN 7F273) go in the three grooves (at the bottom of this photo). A lone sealing ring (PN 87054-S96) goes in the top groove. Give these rings and grooves abundant lubrication.

12 Install Direct Clutch Sealing Rings

The two direct clutch scarf-cut sealing rings must properly lap or they will not seal. The lap joint must meet head-on and be perfectly aligned. If these seal ends overlap, you get internal leakage.

Reverse Clutch Assembly

1 Install Number-9 Needle Bearing

Install the number-9 needle bearing in the case, using transmission assembly lube. Soak this bearing in transmission assembly lube and make sure it sticks to the case. Make sure it remains centered during installation.

2 Prepare to Assemble Reverse Clutch

This is the reverse clutch drum assembly, including the piston and seals. Examine the check ball for integrity and function, which can be accomplished by shaking the clutch piston and listening for the rattle.

3 Install Reverse Clutch Piston

Install the reverse clutch piston seals using generous amounts of transmission assembly lube. Pay close attention to the seal status. The seal grooves and seals must be hospital clean. Apply uniform pressure to the piston while feeling for a smooth transition.

4 Install Reverse Clutch Piston Snap Ring

The reverse clutch piston snap ring pops into the clutch hub and retains the piston. Check this ring carefully for proper seating. It can pop out if it is not completely seated.

Critical Inspection

5 Install Belleville Spring and Snap Ring

Inspect the reverse clutch Belleville return spring for cracks and distortion prior to installation. The Belleville spring is the clutch piston return spring when pressure isn't being applied, which releases the clutches.

6 Install Reverse Clutch Pressure Plate

Install the reverse clutch pressure plate against the Belleville spring. Check the pressure plate for freedom of movement in the clutch drum.

7 Install Reverse Clutch Plates

Lay the clutch discs and plates into the reverse clutch drum. Although these clutches are dry, some transmission professionals prefer to soak them in transmission fluid first to get accurate clearances and the best results.

8 Install Reverse Clutches

The reverse clutch discs alternate with plates. The plates should have been resurfaced or replaced. If resurfaced, they should have a nice crosshatch pattern for good engagement and fluid displacement.

9 Install Reverse Clutch Rear Pressure Plate

Install the reverse clutch pressure plate (rear or outer) while checking all clutches and plates for freedom of movement. Clutch clearances should be .040 to .059 inch. If this cannot be achieved, go with the appropriate retaining ring: .060 to .064, .074 to .078, .088 to .092, or .102 to .106 inch.

10 Install Retaining Ring

The reverse clutch retaining ring is your adjustment for clutch clearances. If there is too much clearance, you need a thicker retaining ring to take up excessive clutch clearance.

11 Install Number-2 Needle Bearing

Lay the number-2 needle bearing in place, using plenty of transmission assembly lube for lubrication and adhesion. The needle bearing, also known as a Torrington bearing, reduces internal rolling and thrust friction.

First Gear in Drive

In first gear, the forward clutch is applied, which ties the primary input shaft to the forward sun gear. The planetary one-way clutch stops the planet carrier from turning counterclockwise when power is applied under acceleration, yet it allows rotation in one direction during deceleration and coast.

First Gear in Manual 1

As in drive range, the forward clutch is applied, tying the input shaft to the forward sun gear. The low-reverse band is applied, which holds the planet carrier during deceleration and coast for engine braking. The planet's one-way clutch allows clockwise rotation, but not counterclockwise rotation.

Second Gear in Drive

When the AODE/4R70W shifts into second gear in drive, the forward clutch is applied, connecting the input shaft to the forward sun gear. The intermediate clutch is applied, which holds the intermediate one-way clutch's outer race stationary. The intermediate one-way clutch keeps the reverse clutch drum, shell, and reverse sun gear from rotating counterclockwise when power is being applied (acceleration). The planetary one-way clutch overruns.

Second Gear in Manual

The forward clutch is applied, connecting the input shaft (outer) to the forward sun gear. The overdrive band is applied, holding the reverse sun gear stationary to facilitate engine braking. Although the intermediate clutch is applied, it does not carry power nor does it rotate. The planetary one-way clutch overruns.

Third Gear in Drive

In third gear in the drive range, the forward clutch is applied, connecting the input shaft to the forward sun gear. The direct clutch is applied, tying the input shaft to the planet carrier to the smaller inside input shaft (stub shaft). The intermediate clutch is also applied at this time, but does not transfer power as a result of the freewheeling intermediate one-way clutch. The planet's one-way clutch overruns.

Fourth Gear in Drive (Overdrive)

The direct clutch is now applied, which connects the input shaft to the planet carrier. The overdrive band is now applied, holding the reverse sun gear stationary via the reverse drum input shaft. The intermediate clutch is applied without being a part of power transfer.

Reverse Gear and Neutral

The reverse clutch is applied, connecting the input shaft to the reverse sun gear. The low-reverse band is applied, which holds the planet carrier. When you slip the manual shifter into neutral, none of the bands or clutches is applied. Park gives the same result but also engages the parking pawl.

Internal Components Installation

1 Install Low-Reverse Band

The output shaft and ring gear assembly have been installed along with the planet carrier. The planet carrier splines inside the ring gear with gentle back-and-forth twisting to achieve proper engagement.

Documentation Required

2 Assemble and Install Intermediate One-Way Clutch

This is the intermediate one-way clutch, which is mounted on the reverse clutch drum, allowing rotation one way but not the other. Take note of how the rollers fit into the cage. Do not get this backward.

3 Install Intermediate One-Way Clutch

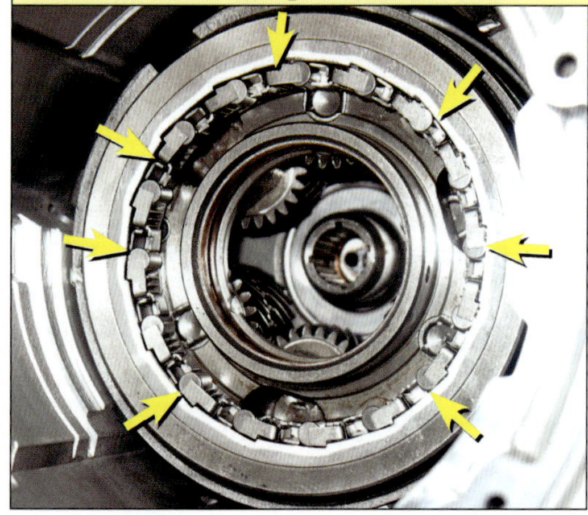

This is the intermediate one-way clutch installed. Note the proper installation and how the rollers are located (arrows). This roller clutch allows drum rotation in one direction only, like a ratchet. Be sure to lubricate the rollers generously.

4 Install Planetary Support Assembly

The planetary support assembly fits into the main case. This center support carries the planet carrier. Use plenty of lubrication on the center support bushing.

5 Install Anti-Clunk Spring

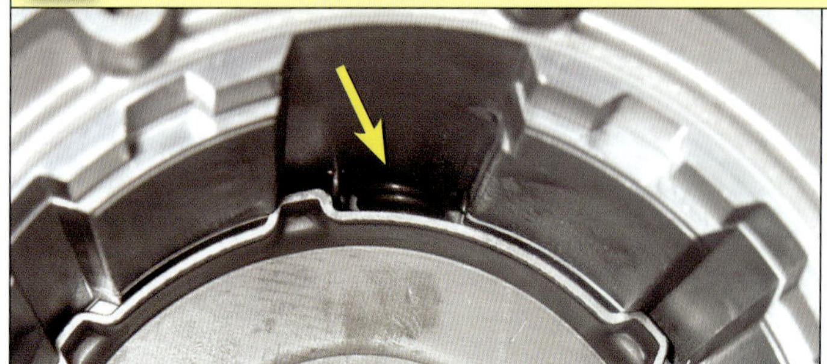

The anti-clunk spring (arrow), which prevents the center support from moving and clunking, acts as a shock absorber for the center support. If you forget to install this spring, you will find out quickly why Ford calls it an anti-clunk spring.

6 Install Center Support Retaining Ring

Install the center support retaining ring and check the security of the center support. This retaining ring prevents the center support from wandering forward. Once this ring is seated, check its security.

7 Install Forward Sun Gear

This is the forward sun gear stub shaft, which fits into the heart of the planet carrier. The number-5 needle bearing is already installed here. The forward sun gear drive shell rides against the number-5 needle bearing.

8 Install Forward Sun Gear Drive Shell Stub Shaft

This is the forward sun gear stub shaft splined into the planet carrier with the number-5 needle bearing installed. All bearing surfaces should have been lubricated.

9 Install Forward Sun Gear Drive Shell

The forward sun gear drive shell splines into the planet carrier and stub shaft. Work the sun gear drive shell back and forth to seat.

10 Install Forward Sun Gear Drive Shell *CONTINUED*

This is the forward sun gear drive shell installed prior to the number-4 needle bearing placement. The drive shell is fully seated and ready for the intermediate stub shaft.

11 Install Intermediate Stub Shaft

The intermediate stub shaft splines into the planet carrier. This shaft operates inside the outer stub shaft. Twist and wiggle the stub shaft and feel for proper seating.

12 Install Number-4 Thrust Needle Bearing

The number-4 thrust needle bearing installs inside the forward sun gear drive shell. Use plenty of lubrication as a pre-lube and for adhesion.

13 Install Forward Clutch Hub

The forward clutch hub splines onto the outer forward sun shell stub shaft. Apply transmission assembly lube on all contact surfaces.

14 Install Number-3 Thrust Needle Bearing

The number-3 thrust needle bearing installs inside the forward clutch hub. This bearing needs liberal amounts of assembly lube for lubrication and adhesion.

Processor Inputs

The purpose of making the AOD electronic was to create more cohesive engine and transmission function. The EEC-IV and EEC-V processors are engineered to operate based on the following inputs:

Throttle Position Sensor (TPS): A variable resistor at the engine's throttle body that controls current flow to ground. It controls spark, fuel, and transmission shift curves based on throttle position and current flow.

Mass Airflow (MAF) Sensor: Contributes to engine and transmission control via air flow and variable resistance.

Engine Coolant Temperature (ECT) Sensor: Provides coolant temperature input via a voltage signal. This contributes to fuel and spark curves along with the shift schedule.

Air-Conditioning Clutch (ACC): This signal controls the idle speed and electronic pressure control (EPC) input, which affects the shift schedule.

Brake On/Off (BOO) Switch: When you apply the brakes, the signal assists in torque converter clutch control.

Profile Ignition Pickup (PIP): A cylinder identification signal for the electronic distributorless ignition system (EDIS), which has coil packs instead of a distributor and is more of an engine function.

Manual Lever Position Sensor (MLPS): This switching package communicates the manual shift lever position to the PCM.

Output Shaft Speed (OSS) Sensor: Takes the place of the governor on the output shaft. It does what the governor did hydraulically. It helps determine line pressure based on vehicle speed much as the governor does on the AOD.

Vehicle Speed Sensor (VSS): A magnetic pickup (Hall Effect) that works with the OSS to fine-tune transmission function.

Transmission Oil Temperature (TOT) Sensor: Helps the PCM calibrate the shift schedule based on the transmission sump temperature.

Processor Outputs

Electronically triggered solenoids are simple electromagnets. They're either on or off or on/off in a duty-cycle (pulse) pattern.

Electronic Pressure Control (EPC) Solenoid: Your AODE/4R70W's pacemaker. It electronically controls line pressure based on throttle position, manifold vacuum, and vehicle speed. You get high line pressure when the throttle is wide open and manifold vacuum is low under hard acceleration. At WOT, you want high line pressure for firm clutch and band engagement.

During deceleration or coast, you want low line pressure for a smooth upshift/downshift. You don't want to feel downshift. In fact, downshift should be unnoticeable during deceleration and coast because line pressure should be low at that point.

Your Ford's PCM allows a given amount of current flow to and from the EPC solenoid based on driving conditions. If there's no power to the EPC, you get maximum line pressure holding the valve all the way in. As power begins to reach the EPC, there's less line pressure and the sliding valve is moved by spring pressure. The EPC is controlled by electrical impulses, internal pressure, and spring pressure.

Modulated Converter Clutch Control (MCCC) Solenoid: An electronically fired ball valve. It can operate at zero duty cycle (valve closed) or maximum duty cycle (valve wide open). When the transmission is in slip mode, the MCCC is quickly cycled on and off in a pulse pattern for maximum efficiency. The MCCC engages and disengages the torque converter clutch.

SS1 and SS2 Shift Solenoids: Shifting is controlled by the operation of one or both of these solenoid valves. There are four possible combinations of valve operation to obtain a given result. The shift solenoids open the shift valves when they receive power. When there is no power, the shift valves are closed. When the solenoids are energized, the valves are open.

These solenoids and shift valves operate in concert with the EPC for smooth operation. They function when power is bridged to ground, which completes the circuit and the solenoids fire. Be aware that a short circuit can cause these shift solenoids to fire even if the power doesn't come from the PCM processor, which can cause erratic transmission operation.

Internal Components Installation *CONTINUED*

1 Inspect Forward Clutch Assembly

This is the forward clutch with input shaft. Examine the check ball valves for freedom of movement. They should rattle when you shake the clutch and shaft assembly.

2 Assemble Forward Clutch Piston

Install the forward clutch piston seals. Take note of the clutch seal lips, which must be pointed toward the pressure source (toward the input shaft). Pressure causes the lip to seal. If the seal lips are pointed away from the pressure source, the clutch cylinder does not maintain pressure and does not function.

3 Lubricate Seals

Important! !

! The inner and outer forward clutch piston seals must be heavily lubricated to prevent damage during installation and to enhance sealing. The seal lip should be pointed toward the pressure source (inside the bore). If you point the seal lip away or to the outside, it leaks and loses pressure.

Special Tool

4 Install Forward Clutch Piston

The forward clutch piston installs using a Lip Wizard. It allows the seals to transition smoothly without binding. Any seal bind is a guaranteed leak. Do a leak check with compressed air.

5 Install Clutch Piston Return Spring

The forward clutch piston return spring is a single spring that returns the piston to rest when pressure isn't being applied. The spring is compressed to make way for the C-clip retainer.

6 Install C-Clip

Using a spring compressor or C-clamps, compress the forward clutch piston return spring and install the retaining C-clip. Make sure the C-clip is secure before moving on.

7 Install Forward Clutch Steels

Alternate the forward clutch plates with clutch friction discs. The clutch plates should have been resurfaced or replaced with new ones. The plates should have a good crosshatch pattern.

8 Install Forward Clutch Discs

Install the forward clutch frictions alternately between the steels. Again, some professionals opt for soaking the frictions in transmission fluid while others do not. It does affect clearances.

9 Install Pressure Plate and Retaining Ring

The forward clutch friction and steel clearances should be .050 to .089 inch. Ring thicknesses are .060 to .064, .074 to .078, .086 to .092, and .102 to .106 inch.

10 Mate Forward and Reverse Clutches

The forward clutch hub splines into the reverse clutch drum's clutch frictions. Rock these assemblies back and forth until the forward clutch is completely seated in the reverse clutch drum.

From Electric to Hydraulic

Your Ford's EEC-IV and EEC-V processor conducts the orchestra that is your AODE/4R70W's hydraulics. Transmission problems are often perceived as mechanical or hydraulic when they are actually electrical issues that adversely affect the hydromechanical parts. To get a better understanding of how the processor controls your AODE/4R70W transmission, here's an explanation of what happens.

First Gear in Drive

In first gear in the drive range, the SS1 is on and the SS2 is off. The MCCC is off (on the torque converter, no lockup). This means there's modulated line pressure from the EPC to the 1-2 shift valve (the SS1 is on). It also means there's no pressure to the intermediate clutch pack. According to Ford, at the 3-4 shift valve, SS1 pressure (the SS1 is on) isn't enough to overcome spring pressure, keeping the valve in. With this sequence of events, pressure goes to the forward clutch pack through the orifice control valve and the 2-3 backout valve.

First Gear in Manual 1

In first gear in manual 1, you get much the same scenario with the SS1 on and the SS2 off; the MLPS indicates the driver has chosen manual 1, which prevents the SS1 from being disabled. This keeps the transmission in first gear. The MCCC is off.

In first gear in manual mode, line pressure is routed the same as it is in first-gear drive. The difference is the SS1 function. The SS1 stays on, keeping the transmission in first gear. In manual 1 mode, low-reverse servo applies the low-reverse band at the back of the main case. Servo apply pressure is control led by the low servo modulator valve.

If you have a malfunction in manual 1, check for power to the SS1 solenoid. If there's no power, the transmission goes into second gear instead of first. If you have no engine braking in manual 1, the problem isn't electronic. Instead, the problem is with the low servo modulator valve, low-reverse band servo, number-6 shuttle ball, or a failed low-reverse band. Begin your troubleshooting with electronics, then mechanicals.

Second Gear in Drive

In second gear in drive range, both the SS1 and SS2 are off. The MCCC is controlled by the PCM. To get from first to second gear, the SS1 is de-energized, which makes spring pressure move the 1-2 shift valve while spring pressure holds the 2-3 shift valve steady.

Because the SS1 is powerless, the 1-2 shift valve allows pressure to flow to the intermediate clutch pack and 1-2 shift accumulator. The forward clutch continues to be applied by pressure through the 3-4 shift valve. Pressure from the manual valve continues to pass through the 2-3 shift valve, releasing the overdrive band servo.

Second Gear in Manual

In second gear in manual range, both the SS1 and SS2 are off. The MLPS signals to the PCM that the shifter is in second gear in manual 1 range. The converter clutch control solenoid is then controlled by the PCM.

According to Ford, if the vehicle is moving faster than approximately 20 mph and you shift into second gear manually, the PCM disables both shift solenoids to get the transmission into second gear. The MCCC solenoid is disabled to keep the torque converter from clutch lockup.

The fluid pressure is the same as second gear in drive range. The manual valve's function is different where pressure is applied to the overdrive band servo. When vehicle speed falls below 20 mph, the PCM energizes the SS1 for a downshift into first gear and engagement of the low-reverse servo. If the SS1 solenoid remains energized or the 1-2 shift valve sticks, you don't get a 1-2 upshift.

Ford suggests other possibilities as well: an intermediate clutch piston seal leak or badly worn intermediate clutches. Another possibility is a leaking 1-2 accumulator cover or piston seal. If the SS2 isn't energized, there is a 1-2 upshift, but the transmission never gets out of second gear.

Third Gear in Drive (Overdrive)

In third gear in overdrive range, the SS1 is off and the SS2 is on. The MCCC gets pulsing signals from the PCM. As the AODE/4R70W shifts

Troubleshooting

Are you looking at potential electronic control issues? For example, the SS1 solenoid doesn't get power and you start off in second gear. Another scenario with a failed SS1 is starting in first gear and going immediately to overdrive. Ford says that if you have no forward gear, the problem is likely the transmission, not the electronic control.

Begin your troubleshooting with electronics, the most frequent problem. Then check the hydraulic control. And finally, check the raw mechanicals of the geartrain. ■

into third gear, the output shaft sensor signals the PCM to energize the SS2, which directs pressure to the 2-3 shift valve and ultimately the 3-4 shift valve. The 2-3 shift valve moves under pressure against spring pressure. The 1-2 shift valve remains as is.

Pressure flows to the direct clutch and the 2-3 accumulator through the 2-3 backout valve. Pressure all by itself doesn't move the 3-4 upshift valve. As a result, Ford engineers added a spring to give the 3-4 shift valve a helping hand. The 2-3 backout valve, as the name implies, regulates the feel of a 2-3 upshift. With light throttle pressure, the 2-3 backout valve applies fluid under pressure via an orifice. Put the pedal to the metal and fluid under pressure flows through a different orifice to apply greater pressure.

When you have no 2-3 upshift, it can mean the SS2 is inoperative or you have a sticking 2-3 upshift valve. Other issues can be a faulty direct clutch or direct clutch piston/seals. If you get a harsh 2-3 upshift, the problem is likely the 2-3 accumulator or excessive line pressure.

Internal Components Installation *CONTINUED*

1 Install Forward and Reverse Clutch Assembly

The forward and reverse clutch assembly installs in the main case. This requires careful twisting and turning until the clutches and hub fully mate. Also install the input shaft sealing rings at this time.

2 Install Overdrive Band

Install a new overdrive band and anchor it to the pin. Line it up for the overdrive band servo piston. Double-check the security of the band at the servo and anchor pins.

3 Prep Overdrive Band Servo Piston

Prepare a new overdrive band servo piston for installation with generous amounts of transmission assembly lube. Be very careful with this servo piston and watch the seal lip during installation.

Special Tool

4 Install Overdrive Band Servo Piston

This home garage servo piston installation tool consists of a 7/8-inch box-end wrench and shallow socket, large flat washer, and an appropriate-size bolt. Use a little leverage to install the snap ring. You may also use the Ford tool (PN T92P-70023-A).

5 Check Band Anchor and Servo Pin Alignment

Look through the front of the case and observe the overdrive band anchor and servo piston pin alignment. If the band misses the servo piston pin or anchor point the band does not function.

6 Stack Intermediate Clutch Steels and Frictions

The intermediate clutch discs and plates stack up like this. Begin with a plate and alternately stack clutch discs and plates. Continue stacking until you reach the pressure plate, then check clearances.

7 Install Top Clutch Plate

Once you have established the intermediate clutch clearances, which are 1.634 to 1.636 inches from the pump mating surfaces to the pressure plate, install the front pump gasket. Adjust clearance via the clutch plates, which are .071 to .067, .081 to .077, .091 to .087, or .101 to .097 inch, using a depth micrometer. The top clutch plate should be your plate.

8 Install Front Pump Gasket

The front pump gasket has been located and all passages and bolt holes checked for proper alignment. Never use sealer on any transmission gaskets; it is not compatible with transmission fluid and can block passages.

Sump Temperature Sensor Values

Check the transmission sump temperature sensor in your troubleshooting. Here are the resistance levels.

Fluid Temperature (degrees F)	*Resistance (ohms)*
32 to 58	37K to 100K
59 to 104	16K to 37K
105 to 158	5.0K to 16.0K
159 to 194	2.7K to 5.0K
195 to 230	1.5K to 2.7K
231 to 266	0.8K to 1.5K

While you're in there, check the harness resistance levels as well.

Fourth Gear in Overdrive

Fourth gear in overdrive range has both the SS1 and SS2 on. The MCCC again gets pulses from the PCM tied to driving conditions. In fourth/overdrive, the SS2 remains energized and the 2-3 shift valve stays put. This allows for a pressure path to the direct clutch (engaged). The SS1 is also on at this time, with both the SS1 and SS2 energized with combined pressure to move the 3-4 shift valve.

Because the 3-4 shift valve has moved, there is no fluid pressure to the forward clutch. Pressure is instead directed to the overdrive servo regulator valve. This allows full pressure to the overdrive servo and band. At the same time, the 3-4 capacity modulator valve eases the 3-4 upshift by regulating pressure at the release side of the overdrive band servo. The forward clutch release pressure unseats the valve body's number-2 check ball (WOT) or through to the FC34 fluid circuit (light or no throttle), which depends on 2-3 backout valve position.

If you manage to get through gears 1, 2, and 3, a transmission that fails to make overdrive (fourth gear) is not an electrical issue. If your AODE/4R70W experiences no 3-4 upshift, it is a sticking 3-4 shift valve, overdrive servo issue, or a failed overdrive band. Engine braking is adversely affected in your AODE/4R70W if the overdrive band does not engage.

Reverse Gear

In reverse, the SS1 is on and the SS2 is off. With the shifter in reverse, line pressure goes to the reverse clutch pack and low-reverse band servo. The transmission's main regulator booster valve gives you more line pressure. Because the reverse clutch pack is engaged only in reverse, you're looking at only the reverse clutch or the reverse fluid circuit in the valve body when there's a malfunction.

Torque Converter Clutch

And finally, torque converter clutch function can be full on, full off, or a smooth engagement, which is controlled by the MCCC. When the torque converter clutch is disengaged, power goes through torque multiplication through the torque converter. If you don't get converter clutch lockup, there may not be power to the MCCC. Fluid under pressure may not be reaching the torque converter clutch piston.

Internal Components Installation *CONTINUED*

1 Replace Front Pump Bushing

Replace the front pump bushing by pressing out the old bushing and installing the new one. Use a bushing driver of the correct size and a press. If you don't have a press, just about any machine shop has one.

2 Install Front Pump Seal

Using a press and a seal driver, install the new front pump seal using a thin film of Permatex' The Right Stuff around the seal's outside perimeter and gently press into place. Generously lubricate the seal lip with assembly lube.

3 Install Intermediate Clutch Piston Seals

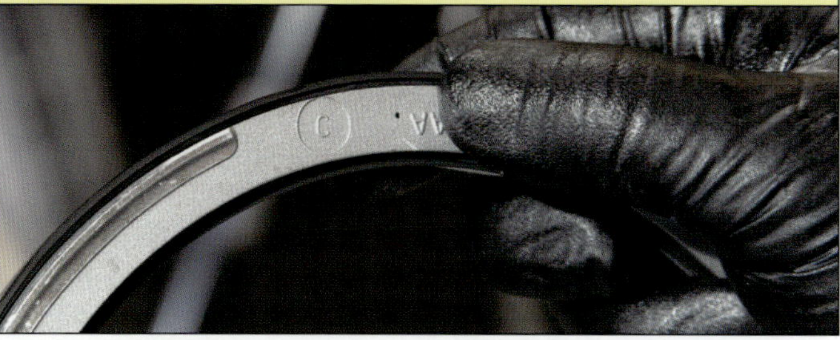

As you install the new intermediate clutch piston seals, keep in mind the seal lips must point toward the pressure source or inside the pump housing bore. Pressure against the seal lip is self-sealing and fail-safe. If you point the seal lip toward the intermediate clutches, you will have an internal hydraulic leak and no intermediate clutch function.

4 Install Front Pump Perimeter Seal

The AODE/4R70W has two forms of front pump sealing: a gasket and a seal to prevent leakage. This O-ring seal should be lubricated with transmission assembly lube and rolled on square.

5 Install Intermediate Clutch Piston

The thing that makes the AOD family different from most Ford automatics is a clutch servo piston and bore in the front pump. Install the intermediate clutch servo piston in the front pump. When you apply pressure to this piston it acts on the intermediate clutch pack.

Special Tool

6 Install Clutch Piston

Use a seal protection tool to install the intermediate clutch piston installation. Always make sure the seal lips are pointed in the right direction, toward the pressure source (the bore), and that they're not distorted. If the seal lip is pointed away from the bore, it does not hold pressure and the servo piston does not function.

7 Examine Intermediate Clutch Pressure Plate

Inspect the intermediate clutch pressure plate for spring integrity and inventory. There should be nine springs in serviceable condition free of distortion. Because these springs are attached to the pressure plate, they should all be present and in serviceable condition.

8 Install Intermediate Clutch Pressure Plate

Check for proper spring alignment and positioning. Check this pressure plate for freedom of movement before installing the pump.

9 Check Pump Rotor Side Clearances

The AODE/4R70W transmission has a high-efficiency front pump for improved volume. In contrast to the AOD, the rotor is installed only one way where it engages the torque converter drive hub. Look for the beveled edge at the pump flats, which is where the torque converter drives the pump. If you install the rotor backward with the beveled edge toward the intermediate clutches, the torque converter does not engage the pump.

Professional Mechanic Tip

10 Pack Pump Rotor Cavity with Assembly Lube

PRO TIP Because you want immediate fluid flow when the engine is fired, pack the pump with assembly lube and transmission fluid for a good prime. You also want to service the torque converter (not shown) with 2 quarts of transmission fluid, which helps prime the pump.

11 Install Front Pump Sealing Rings

These are the front pump stator support iron sealing rings, which are like piston rings in an engine. Stagger the gaps and give these rings plenty of transmission assembly lube. Staggering the gaps helps the sealing rings hold pressure.

12 Assemble Pump Halves

Make sure all holes line up, then mate and secure the pump halves. Before mating them, make sure all contact surfaces are clean. Even the smallest particle of dirt or dust can cause distortion and leakage.

Torque Fasteners

13 Install Bolts and Torque to Spec

Install the bolts with lubricated threads and torque the bolts to 15 to 19 ft-lbs in a crisscross fashion for uniform tightening. Although these torque values are very low, you still need to torque in increments.

14 Inspect Pump Stator Support Sealing Ring Gaps

Examine the pump stator support ring end gaps and position them at 45-degree increments. Staggering these gaps helps contain line pressure at the source. These sealing rings must be well lubricated for pump installation.

15 Install Thrust Washer

Use assembly lube as an adhesive to install the thrust washer. This is the natural color version (.085 to .089 inch). The other four thickness options are green (.050 to .054 inch), yellow (.068 to .072 inch), red (.102 to .106 inch), and blue (.119 to .123 inch).

16 Compare Main Case and Pump Passages

There is only one way to install the front pump. Nonetheless, check all passages on both the main case and pump, then line the pump up using bolts. Lubricate the bolt threads and check the bolt travel. If you encounter any binding, chase the threads and remove the debris.

17 Install Front Pump Assembly

Fit the front pump, then slowly run the bolts down and pull the pump tight. Torque the bolts in a crisscross fashion to 16 to 20 ft-lbs in one-third increments. This allows for proper seating and prevents warping.

Building an AODE/4R70W

Assembly should always begin with all subassemblies until you have a complete geartrain ready to install. Gather all parts on a hospital-clean work surface and organize them into groups of unassembled subassemblies that make up the various components.

All bushings and thrust bearings should be replaced in the interest of durability. Never reuse old bearings or seals. Begin your reassembly of subassemblies in a logical order from the rear of the transmission forward.

Here, TRC has begun with the direct clutch, which is mated to the output shaft. The AODE/4R70W direct clutch is a stronger stamped steel with more clutch surface area for durability and power transfer. The direct clutch should be fitted with new steels and frictions. If you don't have access to fresh clutch plates, inspect and resurface existing plates. If they are heat cracked or bluish, do not reuse them.

Each transmission build shop has its own approach to assembly. TRC installs frictions dry. Others install them wet. Wet frictions allow for more accurate clearances during assembly. Seals and thrusts should be installed wet with transmission assembly lube, though not all shops do it this way.

Closely inspect all hard parts for scoring and cracking. Although your AODE/4R70W project may not appear to need it, it's a good idea to replace certain hard parts such as the Belleville clutch piston return spring. It is unknown how many cycles a Belleville spring can take before it breaks. However, for the sake of longevity, replace yours.

Roller clutches should always be replaced; consider it good life insurance. Rollers become pitted, and this isn't always visible. Cages become damaged and at times this is even harder to see. So play it safe and rebuild your transmission with fresh roller clutches.

While you're building subassemblies, closely inspect planet gears and bushings for abnormal wear and scoring. Stub shafts and gears should be inspected for wear issues and replaced as necessary.

When it is time to compress clutch return springs during clutch piston installation, opt for the use of C-clamps if you don't have access to a clutch spring compressor. As you mate clutch assemblies, ensure complete mating and seating before loading each assembly into the case.

Band assemblies, such as clutches, can be installed wet or dry. Installing them wet gives them a good start against freshly resurfaced clutch drums. Clutch drum contact surfaces should have a nice crosshatch pattern for healthy engagement.

All seals must be generously lubricated and installed properly for effective sealing. A seal lip pointed the wrong way is a guaranteed leaker. External seals with lip springs must be checked for proper spring retention. If the spring is missing and cannot be found, replace the seal.

Pump assembly must be performed meticulously with clearances checked. If there are no serious signs of rotor or cavity wear, the pump can be returned to service. Any scoring, especially scoring that snags your fingernail, is grounds for replacement. Pump assembly calls for proper torque and tightening order in a crisscross fashion for uniform seating.

TECH TIP

Low-Reverse Band Servo Piston Installation

Low-reverse band servo piston installation takes careful thought and attention. A servo piston selection tool (PN T80L-77030-A) bolts to the case above the servo bore to ascertain band torque against the drum. Tighten the center bolt to 50 ft-lbs.

Then, using a dial indicator positioned at the piston and zeroed, back the bolt off slowly until the piston movement stops. Your dial indicator reading should be .112 to .237 inch. If it isn't, you need one of three piston types: one-groove, 2.936 inches; two-groove, 2.989 inches; or three-groove, 3.043 inches, which is the measurement from piston surface to the end of the rod. ■

Internal Components Installation CONTINUED

1 Install Low-Reverse Band Servo Piston Return Spring

Install the low-reverse band servo piston return spring. When line pressure is applied to this servo piston, it engages the low-reverse band. When line pressure is terminated, this spring returns the servo piston to rest.

2 Install Low-Reverse Servo Piston Cover

Install the low-reverse servo cover and snap ring. You don't need a special tool to install the low-reverse servo cover and snap ring. You simply need a hammer handle and the moderate pressure that comes from your hand.

3 Install 2-3 Accumulator Piston and Spring

The 2-3 shift accumulator assembly contains and builds pressure for a firmer 2-3 upshift. This installs exactly as you see here with a cover and C-clip.

4 Install 2-3 Shift Accumulator

The 2-3 shift accumulator drops into its cavity. Make sure you have plenty of lube and smooth piston travel. Spring pressure here determines shift firmness.

5 Install 1-2 Shift Accumulator

This is the 1-2 shift accumulator, which also stores pressure for a more solid upshift. Generously lube this assembly and install it, along with the cover. During installation, watch the seals and protect them from distortion.

6 Install 1-2 Shift Accumulator CONTINUED

This cover contains line pressure at the 1-2 shift accumulator.

Important!

7 Install Electronic Pressure Control Solenoid

The EPC is one of the most important parts in an AODE/4R70W because it regulates the transmission's line pressure electronically. Not enough line pressure and you get slippage. Too much line pressure and you can break the transmission case.

8 Replace Shaft Seal and Install Manual Shift Linkage

Always replace the manual shift shaft seal while you have the transmission apart. Use plenty of lubrication, then drive the seal in. Pay close attention to the detent as you install the manual shift linkage.

Final Assembly

1 Inspect Valve Body

Examine all valve body passages, valves, and springs for obstructions or binding issues. Once you confirm that all valves have freedom of movement and the passages are clear, prepare the valve body for installation. Air pressure should be applied to serve as a valve function check.

2 Install Valve Body

Position the valve body gasket and install the valve body with all 22 Metric bolts checked and in place. Torque the bolts in a strict pattern to prevent warping. The main control pilot bolts receive 140 to 160 in-lbs (not ft-lbs). Attachment bolts receive 80 to 100 in-lbs (not ft-lbs). Torque the bolts gently in one-third increments, from the inside out. Then re-torque them for a final check.

3 Install Manual Shift Linkage and Manual Valve

The manual shift linkage and manual valve line up like this. Park is the last manual detent when the linkage is full forward. The MLPS is outside and is tied to the manual shift linkage. It has three alignment holes (slots). When they are lined up, torque bolts to 62 to 88 in/lbs (not ft-lbs).

4 Inspect Solenoids

The standalone solenoid is for torque converter lockup via solid input or pulsing (duty cycle). The twin solenoids are shift solenoids that are on/off only with either each on or both on, depending on the shift timing.

5 Install Harness

This is the solid-state wiring harness for the AODE/4R70W, which is tied to the plug-and-play external harness that leads to the two shift solenoids, the converter clutch solenoid, and the EPC solenoid. The harness protects the wiring.

6 Install Filter Assembly

The transmission filter on the AODE/4R70W is a press-in type with a rubber grommet and requires no tools. Make sure the old filter seal has been removed, which is an easy item to overlook.

7 Install Output Shaft Extension Housing Bushing

The extension housing received a new bushing. This drain hole must be at 6 o'clock. Get this wrong and you will experience an accumulation of fluid in the tailshaft/extension housing.

8 Install Extension Housing Output Shaft Seal

After you add liberal lubrication to the output shaft seal, press it in. Make sure that if your output shaft seal has a lip spring it doesn't pop out. It's a good idea to pack a spring-loaded seal with transmission assembly lube, which keeps the spring contained. Lose the spring and you will have slip-yoke leakage.

Performance Tip

9 Install Housing Gasket

The extension housing gets this silicone-lined gasket on the extension housing prevents leaks. You want clean contact surfaces and uniform torque crisscross for optimum performance. Torque the gasket bolts to 107 to 132 in-lbs, not ft-lbs. Torque the extension housing bolts to 16 to 20 ft-lbs.

Troubleshooting

Troubleshooting the AODE/ 4R70W begins with ascertaining the problem. Did it come on all at once or did it arrive gradually? Does it happen in one gear range or in all? Did the problem arise after transmission service or part replacement?

Ford recommends the following steps when troubleshooting:

- Verify the problem (what is it doing?).
- Check the vehicle (visually inspect the vehicle).
- Perform a function check (test-drive).
- Review service information such as Technical Service Bulletins (TSB).
- Diagnose the problem (accurately diagnose).
- Repair and verify the repair/ correction.

Ford also recommends performing your troubleshooting step-by-step so you never miss a critical step that could lead you right to the problem. Do not take shortcuts. Begin with the simplest, most commonsense issues. Ford recommends the following, which can be performed with the transmission in the vehicle:

- Check for leaks.
- Focus on any electronic add-on components.
- Are there any vehicle modifications?
- Is the shift linkage properly adjusted?
- When does the malfunction happen?

Fluid Condition

Pull the dipstick and check the fluid condition and level. The fluid color should be reddish-pink. If it is brown or otherwise dark in color that is a clue. Darkness indicates contamination and overheating. It means you have friction material in the fluid as well as burned fluid from slippage and overheating. The fluid condition is your first indication of transmission health. When you check the transmission fluid, it should be checked with the engine running at operating temperature (150 to 170 degrees F).

Electrical Connections

Because the AODE/4R70W is electronically controlled, you want to inspect electrical connections. Another item we never think of

Torque Specifications

Ford stresses tightening bolts from the inside out beginning with the two largest pilot bolts, then the four cover plate bolts, and last, the 12 smaller bolts. Torque in one-third increments until maximum suggested torque is achieved.

Component	Torque
Valve Body to Case	Main, 140 to 160 in-lbs (tighten first); Others, 80 to 100 in-lbs (tighten last)
Pan Bolts	107 to 132 in-lbs
Pump to Case	16 to 20 ft-lbs
Pump Halves	15 to 19 ft-lbs
Tailshaft Housing	16 to 20 ft-lbs
Manual Shift Shaft	20 to 27 ft-lbs
Manual Shift Sensor	62 to 88 in-lbs
Output Shaft Sensor	62 to 88 in-lbs
Output Shaft Housing	16 to 20 ft-lbs

while troubleshooting is what we cannot see that affects the PCM's performance: electromagnetic interference, a close lightning strike, nearby electrical equipment, and even your cell phone or other electronic device. Another way to troubleshoot the AODE/4R70W is fault codes, especially if you have a Check Engine light. Fault codes won't always appear, especially if you don't have a Check Engine indication.

Shifting Problems

Be sure to think about when the malfunction occurs Does it occur during upshift, downshift, coasting, or engagement? Is it a noise or vibration? Is the noise or vibration in rhythm with the engine, driveline, or wheels? Does the engine stall when the transmission selector is placed in gear? What is the engine idle speed? Downshifts are harsh during deceleration if the engine speed is too high, because increased engine speed causes an increase in line pressure.

If you place the selector into gear and there is no engagement in any gear, the first thing you need to do is check the fluid level. If the fluid level is normal and the fluid color is good, the next item to check is the line pressure via the main pressure port. Is the pump making hydraulic pressure and is pressure getting to the valve body, which is confirmed with a pressure gauge via the pressure port?

While you're at it, check the manual shift linkage and manual shift valve. Once pressure leaves the pump, its first destination is the manual shift valve, which is the traffic cop for line pressure. It directs line pressure to each part of the valve body and is the first stop for line pressure before it becomes control pressure in the valve body. Ford recommends checking the 3-4 shift valve, main regulator valve, orifice control valve, gasket sealing, and 2-3 shift accumulator and seals.

Line Pressure

Can't get reverse gear? Check the fluid level and line pressure. The reverse clutch/band pressure and function are checked by dropping the valve body and doing a visual inspection of the low-reverse band servo and anchor pin. It can also mean reverse clutch piston seal problems.

Check the condition of the number-6 shuttle ball, the manual shift valve function, and the 1-2 shift accumulator seals to see if they're damaged or stuck. Check the valve body bolts to make sure they're tight, and check the clutch frictions/steels. All of these items are checked by dropping the valve body and visually inspecting them.

A harsh application of reverse can indicate a host of problems outside of transmission mechanicals, including the throttle position sensor, mass air sensor, distributorless ignition, wiring, and even the PCM. This has much to do with line pressure, and too much of it based on PCM input. Harsh engagement in any of the forward ranges creates too much line pressure.

Weak or soft engagement in any gear indicates insufficient line pressure from the source or leakage at clutch pistons or band servos. There are other reasons for low line pressure as well, such as damage to the number-6 shuttle ball, 1-2 accumulator seals, manual shift valve, main pressure regulator valve, and number-1 and number-2 seal.

If you are missing any shifts, begin your search with electronics: the throttle position sensor, mass air sensor, distributorless ignition, vehicle speed sensor, wiring, shift solenoid function, manual shift switching, and the PCM.

Shift Position Resistance

Check the MLPS, which communicates the manual shift position to the PCM.

Shift Selector Position	***Minimum Resistance (ohms)***	***Maximum Resistance (ohms)***
Park	3,770	4,607
Reverse	1,304	1,593
Neutral	660	807
OD	361	442
2/D	190	232
1	78	95

Improved Input Shaft

In 1998, Ford began fitting the 4R70W with a mechanical-diode intermediate one-way clutch and improved input shaft for greater durability. If you're building an early AODE or 4R70W (prior to 1998), consider upgrading to the mechanical diode and input shaft for improved durability. ■

Torque Converter

Is the torque converter doing its job? Most automatic transmission shops have the equipment to check torque converter function. The transmission must be removed to check torque converter function.

Front Pump

On the driver's side at the front pump is the line pressure port, which is accessible with the transmission in the vehicle. Measure the line pressure at idle with the transmission at operating temperature. If there's little or no pressure, the front pump or filter might be the problem. Remove the pan and inspect the filter. If the fluid and filter are clean, the pump and pressure relief are the next order of business.

Begin the pump inspection by verifying the bolts are torqued correctly and the stator support is secure. In other words, are the two pump halves securely tightened?

The next items to check are the number-3 and number-4 sealing rings. The gaskets and seals are also potential leak and pressure-loss points.

An AODE/4R70W not going into gear could mean problems with the forward clutch piston sealing and check balls. Yet another issue could be the low-reverse one-way clutch.

Clearances

Reverse Band Measurements

Measured with a dial indicator
Suggested depth: .112 to .237 inch

Piston Rod Length (inches), Number of Grooves

2.936, 1
2.989, 2
3.043, 3

Direct Clutch Retaining Ring Thicknesses

Measured with a thickness gauge
Clutch Clearance: .060 to .091 inch

Retaining Ring Sizes (inch)

.050 to .054
.064 to .068
.078 to .082
.092 to .096

Reverse Clutch Retaining Ring Thicknesses

Measured with a thickness gauge
Clutch Clearance: .040 to .059 inch

Retaining Ring Sizes (inch)

.060 to .064
.074 to .078
.088 to .092
.0102 to .0106

Intermediate Clutch Steel Plates

Measured with a depth micrometer at pump mating surface
Clutch Clearance: 1.634 to 1.636 inches

Steel Thicknesses (inch)

.067 to .071
.077 to .081
.087 to .091
.097 to .101

Forward Clutch Retaining Ring Thicknesses

Measured with a thickness gauge
Clutch Clearance: .050 to .089 inch

Retaining Ring Sizes (inch)

.060 to .064
.074 to .078
.086 to .092
.102 to .106

Thrust Washer Identification

Measured with a depth micrometer in two locations
180 degrees apart at pump mating surface

Depth (inches)	Washer Number	Thickness (inch)	Color
1.5033 to 1.4856	1	.050 to .054	Green
1.5213 to 1.5034	2	.068 to .072	Yellow
1.5383 to 1.5214	3	.085 to .089	Natural
1.5553 to 1.5384	4	.102 to .106	Red
1.5803 to 1.5554	5	.119 to .123	Blue

AODE/4R70W Shift Kits

Shift improvement kits are considered mainly for improving performance. However, they also give an AODE/4R70W greater longevity because they reduce and even eliminate slippage, allowing clutches and bands to engage with a minimum of deterioration. And while clutches and bands are making solid engagement and doing their jobs, more power is getting to the drive wheels.

Few companies know more about shift improvement than TransGo, which has been serving automatic performance enthusiasts for more than a half century. The SK AODE Shift Kit by TransGo, designed for the AODE and 4R70W/4R75W, is engineered to eliminate slippage, harshness, and excessive wear in your AODE/4R70W-series transmission. Shift kits reduce wear and tear by firming up and improving shift timing via increased line pressure.

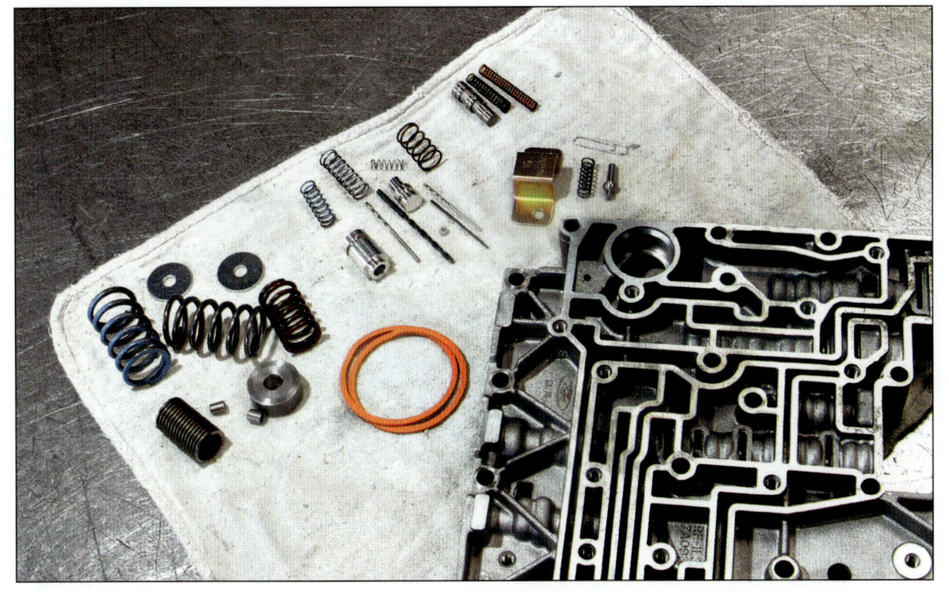

This is the TransGo SK AODE Shift Kit for all 1991–2007 AODEs, 4R70Ws, and 4R75Ws. The SK AODE kit eliminates slippage and damaging harsh shifts. It improves both shift firmness and timing. The SK AODE kit changes the 4-2 downshift to a 4-3-2 downshift, which prevents roller clutch failure. It also improves overdrive band and forward clutch engagement via increased line pressure.

"Line pressure" is transmission tech talk for hydraulic pressure made by the front pump, which is driven by the spinning torque converter, which is tied to the engine's crankshaft and flexplate. When the engine is running, your transmission's hydraulic system is alive with line pressure.

A shift improvement kit is engineered to change line pressure control strategy, which means how clutches and bands engage and with how much control pressure. When line pressure is channeled into the valve body, it becomes control pressure. Because shift improvement kits vary, it is important to understand the differences. There are mild street shift improvement kits that increase control pressure to give you a firm shift and yield more transmission life. There are tow-vehicle shift kits that not only firm the shift, but allow your transmission to go further in a given gear range before upshift occurs. And there are all-out race-oriented shift improvement kits that jar your teeth, smacking clutches and bands with super-firm engagement for uninterrupted power transfer to the rear axle.

The TransGo SK AODE Shift Kit approach to shift improvement is based on a tremendous amount of research and development. TransGo says it developed this kit due to repeated complaints about shift quality from AODE and 4R70W performance enthusiasts. Excessive slippage and parts breakage led TransGo to develop a system that increases line pressure and shift timing, along with reduced harshness at WOT.

The SK AODE Shift Kit changes the AODE/4R70W high-speed downshift from 4-2 to 4-3-2 before the engine and torque converter have time for a runaway that ultimately shatters the one-way roller clutch. This kit also improves clutch fluid loss that damages the overdrive band and forward clutch.

Document Assembly

Disassemble the valve body one valve assembly at a time and arrange each in alignment with its cavity. Take detailed pictures of each valve assembly and the valve body assembly as a whole. Do the necessary machine work (drilling), then thoroughly wash the casting and blow it out with compressed air before assembly. ■

Proper Lubricants

Use a thin film of transmission assembly lube to hold gaskets, check balls, and other small parts in place during assembly. Use transmission fluid on valve assemblies and check each valve for freedom of movement. ■

While your AODE/4R70W is apart, TransGo recommends using its special forward clutch sealing rings with the chamfer side away from the fluid feed hole.

Whether you are using a TransGo shift improvement kit or another from B&M, TCI Automotive, LenTech, Baumann Engineering, or Performance Automatic, follow the instructions to the letter and never mix up the kits interchange components from one kit to another. Each is unique to its manufacturer and has been developed to operate accordingly.

When it is time to road-test your vehicle, take note of the shift-points and vehicle speed. Watch the shift-points during throttle tip-in. Observe the downshift-points and the harshness. You should not be able to feel downshifts if the shift improvement kit has been properly engineered and you have installed it correctly.

Disassembly

1 Disassemble Valve Body

Remove the cover plate, taking note of where each bolt is. Take pictures as you go regardless of what you have for detailed instructions. You need to know how it all went together before it is taken apart. Lay everything out as it came out of the valve body and take detailed pictures.

Critical Inspection

2 Remove Shift Valve Assembly

Remove the shift valve assembly. Inspect the shift valves, also known as shift solenoids SS1 and SS2. Replace the seals on both valves.

3 Remove Converter Clutch Solenoid

Remove the MCCC. Replace the seals. While you're holding this part, closely inspect the solenoid and valve. Look for discoloration at the solenoid, which indicates overheating and warrants replacement.

4 Lift Off Cover Plate

Remove the valve body cover plate and inspect the passages for contaminants. This is the time to take pictures of this side of the valve body before flipping it over and disassembling the other side.

5 Inspect Valve Body

The valve body inspection reveals a complex maze of passages. This is the side facing the pan with the filter and solenoids. There are no check balls in this side.

6 Remove Stiffener Plates

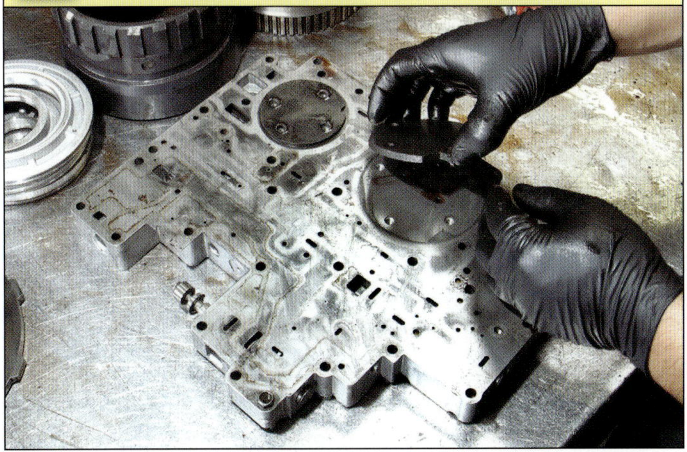

This is the plate that faces the transmission case. Take pictures as you go and be mindful of where fasteners go. Remove these stiffener plates, which are also fluid passages.

7 Lift Off Separator Plate

Carefully remove the separator plate, making sure you do not disturb any of the check balls and other small parts inside. Take pictures of the check ball locations and examine the passages for contaminants.

8 Remove Valve Body with Separator Plate

Once the separator plate is removed, examine the valve body passages and take a picture before disassembly begins. Take note of where all the check balls and other small parts are located (arrows).

9 Remove Filter Screen

Remove this tiny filter and either replace or reuse it. If reused, it must be cleaned. This filter is designed to trap contaminants and keep them out of the valve body passages and valve assemblies.

10 Remove Drainback Valve

This drainback valve is temporarily removed during shift kit installation. The drainback valve is there to keep fluid from leaving the torque converter and overfilling the transmission sump.

11 Inspect EPC Relief Valve

TransGo provides an EPC pressure relief valve, which corrects uncontrolled line pressure if there is an electrical malfunction, sticking EPC valve, or cross-leakage. It also prevents accidental neutral and reapply that can break the one-way roller clutch or stub shaft. The paper clip is used for installation only and is removed once the EPC relief valve is installed.

Shift Accumulator Installation

1 Install 2-3 Shift Accumulator

TransGo says if you have an aluminum piston and the hole in the small end is deeper than the large end you should use the blue spring. If the hole in the large end is deeper, use the washer with the red spring, then install the spacer in the large end. If you have a steel piston, use the blue spring.

2 Install 2-3 Shift Accumulator Washer and Spacer

If you have an aluminum accumulator and the hole in the small end is deeper than the big end, use the blue spring without this washer. If the hole in the big end is deeper, lay this washer in the accumulator piston and use the red spring. If the hole in the bottom of the aluminum piston is deeper than the small end, use the thicker spacer TransGo has provided in the kit at the bottom of the accumulator piston, but not inside the piston.

3 Install Proper Spring

If you go with the solid spring and the blue spring per TransGo's instructions, lay the washer in first (as shown here).

4 Install 2-3 Shift Accumulator Cover and C-Clip

Once you have the right combination of 2-3 shift accumulator springs and washer/ spacer in the bore, install the cover and verify the proper seating of the C-clip.

5 Install Tapered Orifice

Discard the factory's thimble-shaped filter and install one of two provided tapered orifices included in the kit. You want a snug fit but you don't want distortion, so be very careful when driving this orifice in place.

Separator Plate Modification

1 Mark Separator Plate

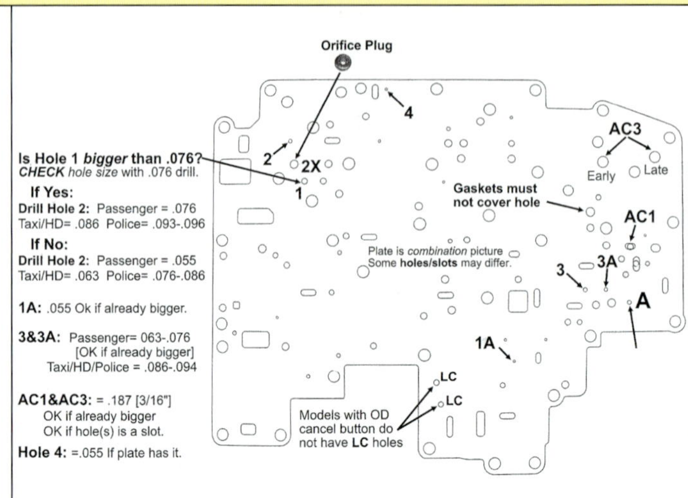

Drill/modify the separator plate per the included TransGo illustration. Keep in mind no two shift improvement kits are engineered the same way, so don't think you're going to outsmart the teacher on this one. Follow your manufacturer's instructions closely and mark everything carefully before you drill. (Illustration Courtesy TransGo)

2 Modify Plate Holes

Enlarge the holes per the marking (here to 0.093 inch) and TransGo instructions with drill bits provided. This is why you must mark the separator plate and circle the holes beforehand. You will learn from the instructions where to drill and what size to drill with the drill bits included in the kit. TransGo provides four bits in this kit: .125, .076, .063, and .055 inch. However, police and taxi applications need .093 to .096 or .076 to .086 inch, depending on which kit you have.

3 Clean Up Holes

Chamfer each hole with a larger drill bit for a clean passage before moving on to the next hole to be drilled. This can be a needle-in-a-haystack environment, which is why you should drill and clean up these holes one at a time.

4 Install Orifice Plug

Install the aluminum orifice plug. Squarely hit the plug with a hammer so it is flush, which secures the orifice plug. This task is nothing more than resizing the hole in the plate.

5 Drill Orifice Plug

Drill the orifice plug with the .055-inch drill bit provided. This resizes the .076-inch hole to .055 inch. This level of modification almost makes you wonder why they just don't include new pre-modified separator plates.

6 Continue Separator Plate Modifications

Modifications vary depending upon the engineering level of your AODE or 4R70W unit type. This is why sometimes kit manufacturers want to know your vehicle identification number or build date when you order the kit.

7 Wash Separator Plate

Wash the separator plate once all modifications are made. Closely examine your work and make sure all holes have been cleaned up and have smooth edges. Make sure these holes and the plate are free of debris.

Valve Body Modification

1 Mark Valve Body for Modifications

Carefully mark the valve body for modification per the TransGo instructions. Double-check the instructions before making any modifications. These modifications mandate extreme attention to detail and a steady hand. Mark and check twice, cut once.

2 Modify Overdrive Servo Regulator Valve

One type of overdrive regulator valve has no hole in the separator plate, which is when you reuse the original spring. If there is a hole in the separator plate, install the blue spring. Also install the provided bushing in this location.

3 Remove Overdrive Servo Regulator Valve

Remove the overdrive regulator valve and lay it out in the order it was installed. Take pictures as you remove each valve assembly.

4 Inspect Overdrive Servo Regulator Valve

Type 1 and Type 2 valve bodies are determined by check ball location, which is confirmed in your TransGo instructions. If your Type 1 valve body separator plate does not have a hole "A," reuse the original spring. If it does have a hole "A," install the blue spring from the kit. If you have a Type 2 valve body, install the bushing (arrow) from the kit, keeping the original valve and spring.

5 Install Overdrive Servo Regulator Valve

There are two potential overdrive regulator valve configurations, depending upon your application. One application calls for using the original spring. The other calls for using the blue spring in the kit.

6 Reinstall Overdrive Servo Regulator Valve Retainer Clip

Reinstall the overdrive regulator valve retainer clip. Air check the valve operation using compressed air. The valve should move back and forth with air pressure application.

7 Remove Main Pressure Booster and Regulator Valves

Remove the main pressure booster and regulator valve assembly and lay these parts out on your work surface. Take pictures of these valves as they came out of the valve body.

8 Remove Main Booster Sleeve, Valve, and Regulator Valves

Here's the main booster sleeve, valve, and regulator valve as factory installed with a blue spring. The TransGo kit offers options, depending on anticipated driving conditions. The specifics are in the instructions. Replace the blue spring with TransGo's white spring.

9 Verify Idle Booster Spring Application

This is the TransGo police/taxi main booster/regulator valve configuration with a white idle booster spring and special booster valve with factory booster sleeve. Unless you're building an AODE/4R70W for police/taxi operation, this valve requires no modification. However, it should be removed for cleaning purposes when the valve body is disassembled.

10 Drill Hole

Drill a .043 to .055-inch hole at the main booster/regulator valve location. Double-check the proper drilling location before you drill. Thoroughly wash the valve body and blow it out with compressed air before reassembly.

11 Reinstall Main Pressure Booster/Regulator

The main pressure booster/regulator valve and sleeve installs per TransGo instructions. Check the valve and sleeve for smooth operation with compressed air. Compressed air acts on the valve as fluid would in actual operation.

12 Reinstall Main Pressure Booster/Regulator *CONTINUED*

Install the pressure regulator valve, then the spring, followed by the small booster valve and the aluminum pressure regulator valve piston.

13 Install and Seat Booster/ Regulator Clip

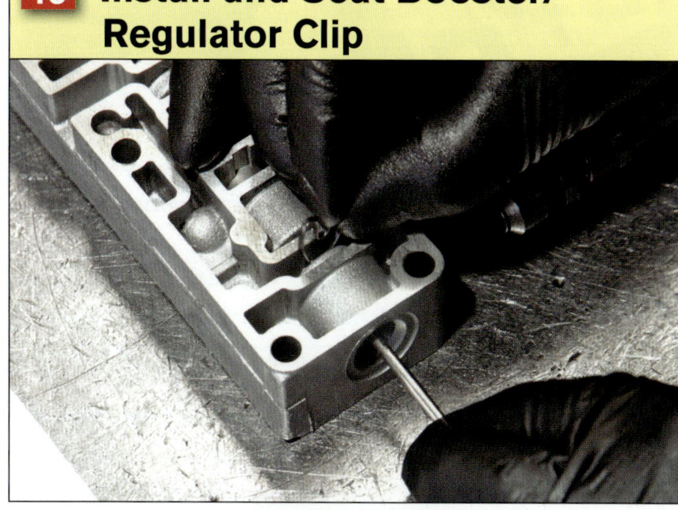

Install the main pressure booster/regulator clip and check it for smooth operation with compressed air. All valves should be checked for freedom of movement and operation this way. Then install the retaining clip.

Bypass Clutch Control Valve Modification

1 Remove Bypass Clutch Control Valve

Beginning with this retaining clip, remove the bypass clutch control valve. Organize this assembly on the bench as it came out and take pictures.

This is the bypass clutch control valve as it is installed at the factory. Inspect each of these parts for unusual wear and scoring and replace as necessary.

2 Modify Bypass Clutch Control Valve

Reinstall the bypass clutch control valve piston exactly as it came out, using compressed air to check the valve function. Use transmission fluid on each of these valve assemblies to ensure freedom of movement and proper function.

3 Install Bypass Clutch Control Valve Spring

For 1991–1995 AODE/4R70W applications, reinstall the factory spring. For 1996-up, use this orange spring. For all applications, use the TransGo lockup bushing provided in the kit.

4 Reinstall Bypass Clutch Control Plunger Valve

Reuse the small bypass clutch control plunger valve with the rest of the valve assembly. This plunger fits into the bushing.

5 Reinstall Bypass Clutch Control Valve Clip

Check the bypass clutch control valve for smooth operation using compressed air. Seat it properly and reinstall this clip. Coat the parts with transmission fluid.

Solenoid Pressure Regulator Valve Modification

1 Inspect Solenoid Pressure Regulator Valve

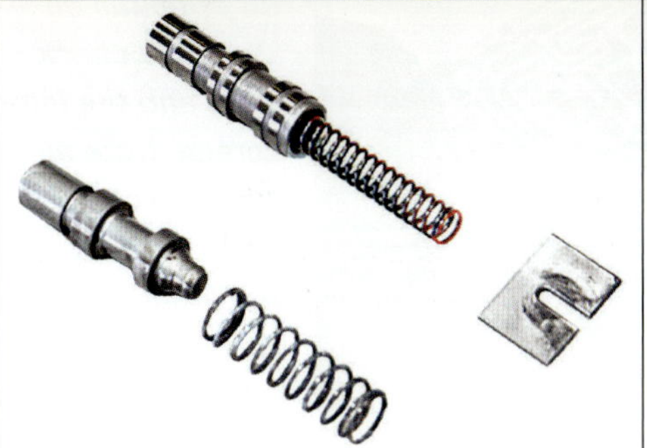

This is the solenoid pressure regulator valve. On the left is the factory configuration. On the right is the TransGo valve with the orange spring. TransGo suggests using the stock spring with the new valve to establish smooth operation, stroking the valve piston at least 50 times with slight side pressure. The valve must fall in and out of the bore smoothly, without any resistance. Once free movement is established, install the valve using the TransGo orange spring.

2 Modify Solenoid Pressure Regulator Valve

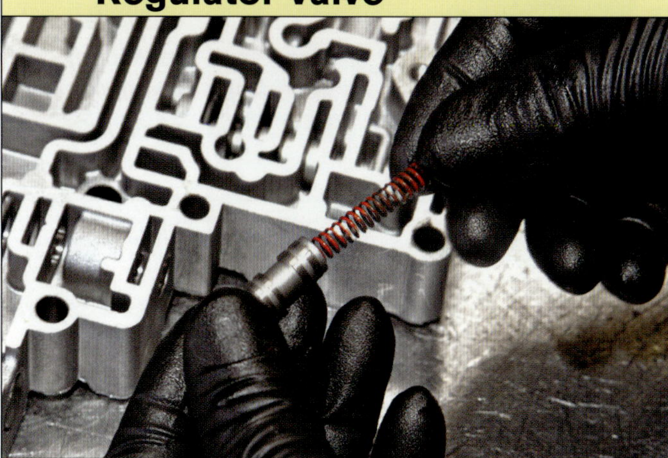

Here's the TransGo solenoid pressure regulator valve piston with the orange spring ready for installation. Verify a smooth fit and use transmission fluid as a lubricant.

3 Install Solenoid Pressure Regulator Valve and Spring

Here's the solenoid pressure regulator valve and spring installed in the valve body. Check the valve for proper operation using compressed air and give it a dose of transmission fluid for smooth function. Seat the valve and spring, then install the clip.

Installation

1 Turn Over Valve Body and Drill Holes

Use caution here, because it is easy to drill in the wrong location. Flip the valve body over and locate the back side of the main pressure booster/regulator valve, which is across from the manual shift valve. Drill two .125-inch holes through this wall. Again, do not attempt this with the valves installed, and always wash out metal debris and blast with compressed air.

Torque Fasteners

2 Install Cover Plate

With a clean valve body, install the cover plate. Remember, the valve body has two plates: the cover (shown) and the separator. Make sure you have all bolts in their proper locations. Torque pin nuts with 13-mm heads to 140 to 160 in-lbs of torque. Torque the smaller 10-mm bolt heads to 80 to 100 in-lbs. Keep in mind this is in-lbs and not ft-lbs.

Documentation Required

3 Install Check Balls and Filter

Install all the check balls and the filter screen. Note all the correct check ball locations and the drainback valve (upper left-hand corner). This is where the photos you took come in handy. You don't want to miss any check balls or have any of them in the wrong location.

4 Install Separator Plate and Gasket

Wipe down the separator plate and gasket to ensure all dust and debris is gone. Even finite dust can cause irregular plate mating and warping. Install the plate and gasket.

5 Inspect and Install Stiffener Plates

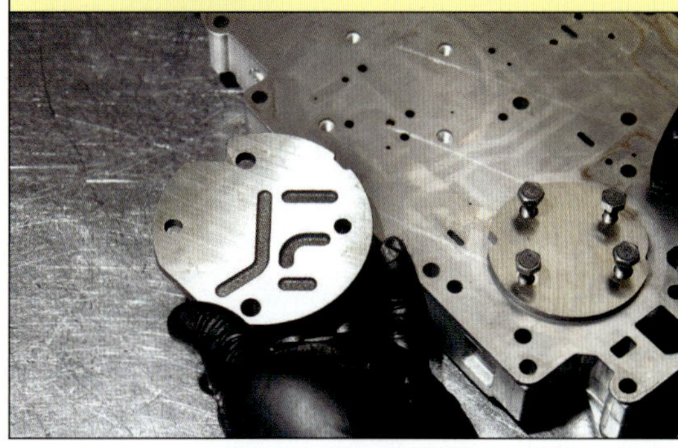

These stiffener plates not only provide structural integrity, they also provide fluid passage through the valve body. Check for clean contact surfaces and install the plates.

6 Tighten and Torque Stiffener Plates

Seat, tighten, and torque the stiffener plates to 71 to 97 in-lbs. Keep in mind this is in-lbs, not ft-lbs, which is an easy mistake to make if you're not paying close attention to what you are doing.

7 Install Valve Body to Main Case Gasket

Check for debris between the main case gasket and the valve body during installation.

CHAPTER 8

Torque Converters

Torque converters are probably the most misunderstood component in an automatic transmission, yet they're the simplest component in both theory and function. A torque converter is a fluid coupling or clutch that slips when the vehicle is stopped and transfers power as engine RPM increases. When the vehicle is in motion and not under acceleration, the torque converter slips and transfers power as vehicle speed decreases. A torque converter, by its very nature as a fluid coupling, also dampens engine combustion pulses to achieve smoother operation. Torque converters have never been considered efficient. They tend to lose more power than they transfer by their very nature as a fluid coupling.

Torque converters don't look like much externally. The action happens on the inside amid the fluid, impeller, and stator. Where torque converters vary most is in pump drive design (locking versus conventional) and stall speed. The AODE and 4R70W differ from the AOD by having a locking torque converter with a clutch. The AOD's lockup occurs in the overdrive unit via the smaller inner input shaft with the split torque feature. The AODE/4R70W has a locking torque converter and a single input shaft.

Torque converters date back more than 100 years. The Germans were among the first to use them in automobiles, trains, and industrial machinery. The first U.S. automaker to use a torque converter was Chrysler in its 1939 Chrysler Imperial, known then as "fluid drive." General Motors followed that act in its 1940 Oldsmobile. Ford then followed suit in 1942 with a BorgWarner automatic in Lincoln and Mercury automobiles.

These early uses didn't go well because there was no torque multiplication. In fact, torque converters were called "fluid couplings" at the time because they didn't multiply torque. General Motors was first with a torque converter that had torque multiplication in the 1949 Buick Dynaflow transmission. Ford joined GM's lead in 1950 with the first Ford automatic transmission designed and manufactured by BorgWarner. GM's legendary mid-1950s Powerglide 2-speed automatic, which was cast iron in those days, become a favorite with drag racers. In fact, the Powerglide remains popular with drag racers today.

Thanks to the basic principles of hydraulics, we put fluid in motion to do our work with a torque converter. Fluid is thrust into motion to drive components in a process known as hydraulics. The same braking system principle that stops your car is what gets it in motion in an automatic transmission. And if everything is working properly, the work is done smoothly and efficiently.

Torque Converter Components

A torque converter consists of five main components.

The impeller, which is tied to the crankshaft puts fluid in motion like a waterwheel in a mill. Fluid is propelled by the engine-driven impeller and thrust through the stator and turbine.

The stator, which directs fluid under pressure to the turbine, channels fluid into turbine blades at high velocity, which is where torque multiplication begins.

The turbine is tied to the transmission input shaft and driven by fluid in motion from the impeller and stator.

The cover (or shell), which is welded to the impeller shell, drives the impeller and gets fluid in motion.

The clutch, which only AODE and 4R70W automatic overdrives have, is applied when the transmission shifts into overdrive. During upshift and acceleration, the torque converter does what it is designed to do: multiply torque.

The cover (or shell) and impeller are welded together to form the main torque converter shell, which drives the transmission's front pump to provide hydraulic pressure for operation and lubrication. The impeller drives fluid through the stator to the turbine, which is tied to the transmission's input shaft. As engine speed increases, fluid flow is directed through the stator to the turbine, which drives the turbine and transmission input shaft to get the vehicle moving.

Stall Speed

The point at which the impeller begins to drive the turbine is known as stall speed. Most stock torque converters "stall" around 1,200 to 1,800 rpm engine speed, which is when the engine really begins to move the vehicle. With a stock torque converter, there is some stall at idle speed because you can take your foot off the brake and get some vehicle motion.

High-performance torque converters stall at higher engine speeds because you want the engine well into its power band when the converter stalls (begins to move the turbine and vehicle). For example, a 2,400-rpm-stall torque converter doesn't really begin to move the vehicle until engine speed reaches 2,400 rpm. The same can be said for a racing converter with a stall speed of 3,600 rpm. You want the engine making power when it hooks up (stalls) with the transmission.

Stator Design

Stall speed is determined mostly by stator design: the blade angle and shape. TCI Automotive explains that the stator is the "brains" of a torque converter because it manages fluid flow from the impeller to the turbine, which drives the transmission's input shaft. This is what makes a torque converter a torque "multiplier." The engine's torque output is multiplied at least twice over thanks to the stator.

In fact, most torque converters multiply torque 2.5:1 times over actual engine torque at stall speed. This doesn't mean you're getting twice the power from your engine. It means fluid under pressure through the torque converter is multiplying your engine's torque only under acceleration until vehicle speed catches up with engine RPM. Within the stator is

The torque converter's stator vectors fluid from the impeller to the turbine for torque multiplication. The one-way clutch allows stator rotation in one direction with the engine's crankshaft.

The basic elements of a torque converter are the impeller, stator, turbine, cover (shell), and one-way clutch. In a locking converter, there is also a clutch and servo. Converters fail mostly due to stator or one-way clutch failure.

The torque converter's one-way clutch allows stator rotation one way, but not the other. When the vehicle is stationary, the stator and turbine are stationary. As the vehicle begins to move, the stator and turbine begin to turn. Under hard acceleration, the stator doesn't turn at the same speed as the impeller and shell. Once vehicle speed stabilizes, the impeller, stator, and turbine all turn at the same speed.

the one-way clutch splined onto the transmission's stator support shaft, which is part of the front pump. The one-way clutch allows the stator to rotate in one direction only with the engine's crankshaft and converter impeller/shell.

The impeller is an integral part of the converter shell, which is driven by the engine's crankshaft. High-performance torque converters have furnace-brazed fins for durability. Many better-quality stock converters are also furnace brazed.

This is a conventional torque converter turbine, which is splined into the input shaft. The turbine gets fluid pressure from the impeller, which is driven by the engine's crankshaft. Fluid travels through the stator into the turbine's fins, which drive the input shaft.

Turbine Motion

Torque conversion or multiplication happens at stall speed with the stator stationary before the turbine begins to move. When the turbine gets under way with the vehicle in motion the stator moves at the same speed as the turbine. You can actually feel this process as you step on the gas and the vehicle accelerates to speed. During hard acceleration, you can feel torque multiplication (stator stationary or slower than turbine speed). As the vehicle gets up to speed, the stator slowly begins to rotate to crankshaft speed. Lean on the gas and stator speed falls behind and torque multiplication comes into play, which is when you feel gut acceleration.

Flow Type

There are two basic types of flow when it comes to torque converters: rotary (circular) and vortex (around the perimeter). When the impeller and turbine speed are uniform, you have rotary flow in a circle around the converter's circumference. If there's a difference in the impeller and turbine speed, flow becomes more vortex (tornado-like).

Prime the Converter

Before installing a torque converter, install at least 1 to 2 quarts of transmission fluid in the converter, which helps prime the converter and pump before engine start. If you install the torque converter empty, you run the risk of immediate pump cavitation on start-up and a dry-transmission hydraulic system, which means you have to drop the transmission and fill the converter or find a way to fill the converter via the front pump and pick-up. ■

Torque Multiplication

As mentioned earlier, the stator helps the impeller and turbine multiply torque. During acceleration, the stator turns at a slower speed than the impeller and turbine, which directs fluid flow more aggressively against the turbine blades.

As vehicle speed catches up with turbine speed, the impeller, stator, and turbine are all whirling at the same speed. Anytime you step on the gas, the stator speed slows momentarily to help direct the fluid and multiply torque.

Torque Converter Function

The AOD does not have a locking torque converter. Instead, the AOD has a torque converter shell that directly turns the overdrive unit known as a split-torque function. Engine power enters the AOD two ways: via the primary input shaft in gears 1–3 and then through the smaller direct input shaft in gears 3 and 4. Even though the AOD does not have a locking torque converter, the torque converter is a direct power path (lockup) in gears 3 and 4.

The AODE and 4R70W have a locking torque converter with a clutch and clutch piston. As the AODE/4R70W enters overdrive, hydraulic pressure is applied to the converter's clutch piston and you have direct lockup with the direct clutch and overdrive.

Consider a Cooler

Because high-stall torque converters create all kinds of heat issues, you should run a transmission fluid cooler as a means to lower operating temperatures. Heat is a very destructive element that can quickly end a transmission's service life. An external transmission cooler can lower fluid temperature dramatically. ■

Choosing a Torque Converter

It is a good idea to discuss your performance needs and expectations with a sales/tech professional before ordering a torque converter. Transmission parts supply houses generally sell stock torque converters with 1,500- to 1,800-rpm stall speeds. These converters are off-the-shelf dead stock pieces not always designed or constructed for performance purposes. Aftermarket high-performance torque converters with the following features can take additional punishment.

- furnace-brazed fins for solid integrity (stock fins are slotted in place, but not brazed)
- dynamic balancing for high-RPM use
- needle bearings instead of thrust washers for reduced friction and increased durability
- heavy-duty stator and sprag/one-way clutch that can take a beating
- generally 400 to 600 rpm over stock stall speed to get the high-performance engine into its power band

Most manufacturers group torque converters by size (usually 11 to 13 inches in diameter) and stall speed (usually 1,200 to 1,800 rpm). As the diameter of a torque converter decreases, stall speed increases, which is why racing converters are generally smaller than street converters. Hookup firmness, stator design, and operating temperature are other factors to consider before you purchase a torque converter.

Stall Speed

Stall is a variable, not a constant, because no two vehicles, transmissions, or torque converters are exactly the same. You can have a 2,400-rpm-stall torque converter that doesn't stall at exactly 2,400 rpm. Another factor influencing stall speed is vehicle weight. Also, you need to consider these questions: Is the vehicle on a hill or on a flat surface? What is the engine's idle speed? Where does the engine make its peak torque and horsepower? How much of a load is the torque converter facing? The 1,200- to 1,800-rpm range is where you want a street engine to begin applying torque. When you slip the transmission into gear, a stock converter provides a gentle nudge as engine torque is applied to the transmission's input shaft and forward clutch. When you have a higher stall speed, that nudge doesn't happen until the engine is closer to stall speed.

You want a higher stall speed on a street engine when torque is expected to come on strong in the 2,400- to 2,600-rpm range. Weekend racers prefer a high-stall torque converter that hooks up in this range because that's where the power is.

Converter Application

Choose a torque converter based on the type of driving you intend to do. A higher-than-stock stall speed doesn't make much sense for the daily commute. For daily drivers, keep stall speed around 1,500 to 1,800 rpm. Weekend Saturday-night drag racers call for 2,200- to 2,600-rpm stall speed. ■

For example, if you have a hot cam and an aggressive induction system, along with a rough idle around 1,000 to 1,200 rpm, you want a higher stall speed for better traffic light idle quality while in gear and the proper application of power as RPM increases. You want the torque converter to take hold (stall) at 2,400 to 2,600 rpm as the engine begins to make power.

Slippage and high-stall speeds affect upshifts. At 5,200 rpm, engine RPM drops 3,500 rpm with each upshift as the transmission moves to a higher gear range. If the converter isn't fully stalled at that point, you lose performance, which is wasted via slippage. This costs you precious time on the quarter-mile or at the traffic light.

Hookup Firmness

Torque converter performance isn't just about stall speed, but about how firmly a converter hooks up when it does stall. This is known as a tight or loose converter. Torque converter manufacturers such as B&M, TCI Automotive, LenTech, and Performance Automatic employ techniques that make torque converters more efficient with less slippage. Much of it is rooted in fluid dynamics and how fluid behaves under given conditions. Because fluid cannot be compressed, it becomes a valuable tool for power transfer via the stator and turbine.

Stator Design

The greatest factor in converter construction is stator design, or the blade/fin shape and angle, which determines stall speed and slippage. It helps determine your quarter-mile times, not to mention the way your Ford behaves on the open road. Choosing a torque converter based on tightness or looseness is a matter of trial and error.

Operating Temperature

Another thing to consider when looking at torque converter stall speed is operating temperature. The lower the stall speed, the lower the operating temperature. There is less pressure involved at lower stall speeds because you're not working the fluid and the converter as aggressively. For street durability and efficiency, you want a lower stall speed. Stall speed is primarily about getting an engine into its power band as the stall comes about.

For stock engines, that power band begins at 2,000 to 3,000 rpm and ramps up to peak torque around 3,200 rpm. Stock torque converters are such that when you put the vehicle in gear, the vehicle creeps with the transmission input shaft catching up to the engine's idle speed. On level ground, you can conceivably get a 1-2 upshift but never see overdrive and converter lockup.

How Torque Converters are Rebuilt

Rebuilding a torque converter requires equipment and a skill set that does not make it practical for the average at-home builder. Also, the convenience and ease of using an aftermarket torque converter supplier makes it impractical to rebuild your own anyway. Still, it's educational to learn about the process of rebuilding and reconditioning torque converters, even though you won't be tackling this project yourself. The following steps are used by Transmission Rebuilding Company (TRC).

Torque Converter Dissassembly

1 Inspect Torque Converter

TRC drains the torque converter and disposes of the fluid responsibly. Next, they cut the shell open at the weld on a lathe such as this.

They dispose of any parts that are not up to standard. Most hard parts are reusable and can be returned to service.

2 Replace Converter Clutch

The torque converter clutches use a friction material similar to the clutches and bands inside the transmission. TRC strips off old friction material and replaces it with new material; they glue it on with a high-strength adhesive.

3 Reface Clutch Contact Surface

The old clutch friction material is removed and new material is installed.

4 Re-Seal Torque Converter Clutch Piston

The torque converter clutch piston works just like the transmission's internal clutch pistons. The piston and bore are inspected and new seals are fitted. The clutch piston gets its pressure via the transmission input shaft. Pressure is modulated by the MCCC solenoid at the valve body.

5 Inspect Stator

This torque converter failure is in the stator assembly of this one-way clutch. The one-way clutch's phenolic cap will be replaced because it is damaged beyond repair and cannot be returned to service.

6 Inspect Stator Cap

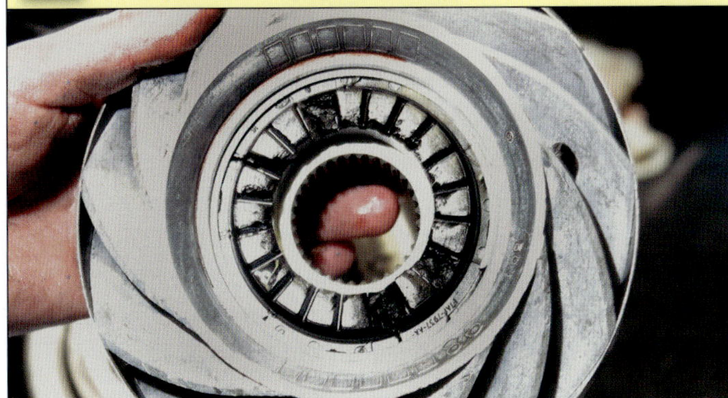

The technician took a closer look at the stator cap and found that it shows extensive damage; it must be replaced. Because the stator cap is subjected to a lot of heat and stress, deterioration isn't surprising. The stator cap will be replaced and the torque converter returned to service.

7 Inspect Impeller Fins

A close inspection of this 4R70W torque converter shows damage to the impeller fins from one-way clutch parts. A converter with this type of damage will be either disposed of or repaired.

8 Inspect Stator One-Way Clutch

As you can see here, the stator's one-way clutch is badly damaged and must be replaced. Damage of this type is from an excessive load and possibly overheating.

Torque Converter Assembly

1 Inspect Torque Converter Clutch

This is a locking torque converter's clutch friction surface, which hooks up with the input shaft for direct drive to the overdrive unit. Clutch engagement happens when the transmission shifts into overdrive.

2 Install Clutch Pressure Plate

This is the converter's clutch pressure plate, which moves and contacts the clutch facing for a direct link to the input shaft. The clutch pressure plate works in a similar way to a manual transmission clutch because it has rebound dampening springs that absorb shock for smoother engagement.

3 Seat Turbine Disc in Converter Shell

The converter's turbine stage is seated in the shell; it's shown here to demonstrate its relationship with the clutch. Thanks to the power of fluid drive, the turbine drives the transmission's input shaft. Fluid under pressure from the impeller is vectored through the stator into the turbine blades. The stator accelerates fluid speed and power, which is how the torque converter multiplies torque.

4 Mate Turbine and Clutch Pressure Plate

The turbine and the clutch pressure plate mate up like this to provide a direct link to the transmission's input shaft. When a driver is on the torque converter's fluid coupling, the connection is smooth between the engine and transmission along with torque multiplication. When the clutch engages, it is more like a manual transmission in high gear: the engine lugs as the throttle is tipped in.

5 Inspect Clutch Disc Rebound Springs

The torque converter clutch works much like a clutch with a manual transmission. These springs are shock absorbers designed to allow the clutch disc to smoothly engage without abrupt engagement.

6 Install Clutch Pressure Plate and Friction Disc

This is the converter's friction disc and pressure plate. It is flipped over and dropped into the shell. The clutch face engages the shell during lockup, and there is a direct link between engine and transmission.

7 Fit Pressure Plate in Converter Shell

This is the pressure plate as it fits into the shell. This is the back side of the clutch's pressure plate, with the front side facing the torque converter's outside shell. When the PCM delivers an electrical signal to the converter clutch's engagement solenoid, line pressure goes to the converter clutch piston, engaging the clutch face and shell for a direct link between the engine and overdrive.

8 Mate Converter Shell and Clutch

Here is how the converter and shell go back together. Once good converter integrity is established, both shell halves will be welded back together.

9 Inspect Torque Converter Clutch Piston

You cannot rebuild your torque converter at home. A transmission shop can rebuild your torque converter or sell you a new or rebuilt converter. Generally, the torque converter clutch piston needs only a seal during a professional rebuild.

10 Inspect Converter Clutch Friction Material

When torque converters are rebuilt, they get fresh parts, including friction material. Old material is stripped off, surfaces are cleaned, and new friction material is glued in place.

11 Dress Converter Hub

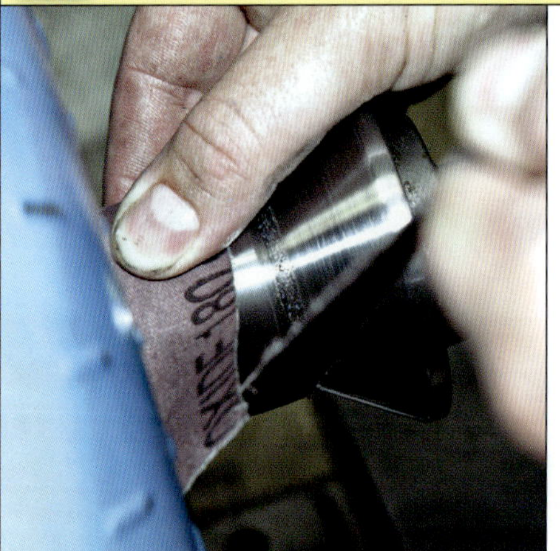

The torque converter drive hub is dressed with fine-grain emery paper to prepare worn surfaces. This process removes burrs and scoring.

12 Inspect Converter Pressure Plates

The locking converter pressure plate on the left provides smoother engagement than the one on the right because the springs are closer to the edge and positioned farther apart.

TECH TIP: Torque Converter Efficiency

Here's a simple formula for determining torque converter efficiency:

RPM = MPH x gear ratio x 336 ÷ tire diameter

Where:
336 is a constant for figuring tire/wheel size and axle ratio

Let's say we're going drag racing and will cross the traps at 117 mph and 5,100 rpm. The vehicle has 3.42:1 rear axle gear ratio with tires that are 27 inches tall.

If you plug the numbers in the formula you get:

117 x 3.42 x 336 ÷ 27 = 4,979

This works out to a difference of about 121 rpm, or 2.4 percent (5,100 actual rpm versus 4,979 formula rpm). This means we have an efficient torque converter because slippage is minimal.

Flash stall is the maximum RPM your engine turns with the brakes applied, vehicle stationary, at WOT. In the example, flash stall happens around 3,600 rpm. Typically, the vehicle overpowers the brakes and begins to move when this happens, making flash stall a difficult number to nail down because vehicle movement allows RPM to rise. ■

13 Weld Torque Converter Together

Once the converter has been checked thoroughly and is ready for a return to service, weld it together with an automatic welder. This is a perfect welding process because it is very consistent.

This is the AOD's duo of input shafts. At first glance, the AOD looks as if it has three input shafts. It actually has two, which makes the AOD different from the AODE/4R70W. The quickest way to identify the AOD's two input shafts is to understand their respective duties.

The smaller shaft is the secondary shaft; it is for overdrive lock-up only at cruise power, which is a light load.

The larger hollow input shaft is the primary shaft for gears 1-2-3 under acceleration, when you are on the torque converter (torque multiplication) before overdrive engagement. The larger shaft is stationary and only supports the torque converter stator.

The AODE/4R70W input shaft is a single shaft with a fluid passage for the torque converter clutch pressure. This AOD redesign made the AOD family simple in function without the need for dual input shafts.

TECH TIP

Converter Installation

Installing an AOD torque converter calls for extraordinary care because you are engaging two input shafts and the front pump drive. Torque converter installation requires some wiggling until you feel the converter engage the inner secondary shaft, outer primary shaft, and stator support: three clunks. If you can fit your hand between the converter and bellhousing, the converter is not properly seated. ■

Incorrectly installing the AOD/AODE/4R70W torque converter is an easy mistake to make. Get it wrong and you trash the transmission's front pump. Rock the converter back and forth. You should be able to feel it seat three times with an AOD and twice with the AODE/4R70W.

With the AOD, you feel the converter slip onto the inner shaft, outer shaft, and the stator support. With the AODE/4R70W, you feel the converter slip onto the input shaft, then the stator support.

INSTALLATION AND ADJUSTMENT

Although transmission installation and adjustment appears straightforward, you should take an orderly, methodical approach to ensure success. You're either swapping in an AOD, AODE, or 4R70W, or you're removing and reinstalling one. Size up the job before you get started and make a checklist of what's needed. Few things are more frustrating than taking your car apart only to discover you're missing crucial parts. Work out a game plan while you still have transportation. And remember, you cannot afford mistakes during installation and break-in. Errors can mean expensive damage because you missed important adjustment techniques.

The most common transmission swap with older Fords is from a C4, C6, or FMX to an AOD or manual 5-speed. The focus here is putting a Ford AOD into a classic Mustang and other vintage Ford applications, which are the more common swaps. If you're going from a C4 to an AOD with a small-block V-8 application, it is important to understand the differences between them. If you're going from a C6 to an AOD in a big-block application, the differences are even more significant because you're going to need an adaptor kit.

Adaptor kits are available for both the FE- and 385-series Ford big-blocks. Keep in mind these adapter kits alter the transmission mount location by 1 to 2 inches toward the rear of the vehicle. An AOD behind an FE or 385 makes the transmission package 1 to 2 inches longer because you're adding 1 to 2 inches to the bellhousing through the thickness of the adapters.

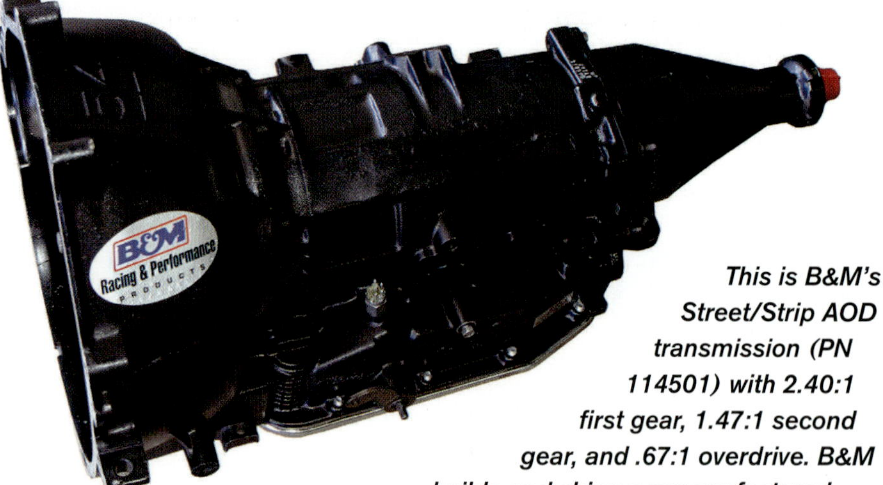

This is B&M's Street/Strip AOD transmission (PN 114501) with 2.40:1 first gear, 1.47:1 second gear, and .67:1 overdrive. B&M builds and ships a remanufactured AOD transmission with new clutches and bands, seals, and any hard parts as needed, including bushings, bearings, and roller clutches. These transmissions are factory calibrated and ready for operation. All you need to do is service them with fluid and a new B&M torque converter. Don't forget proper TV cable adjustment. Be prepared to change the manual shift linkage around to fit your application if needed.

Swapping in the AOD

Because the AOD is longer than the C4, you need a special crossmember and related parts available from suppliers such as California Pony Cars, PATC, Mustangs Plus, California Mustang, and a host of others if you have a vintage Mustang or Cougar. The kit consists of the crossmember, transmission mount, TV cable, shift

Old transmission removal means being prepared with fluid drainage from both the sump and the torque converter. Disconnect the driveshaft, shift, and kickdown linkages. Have a solid means of support beneath the transmission.

Remove the dust cover to get at the torque converter and flexplate. Remove the torque converter fasteners with a 5/8-inch socket. Rotate the engine crankshaft to get at hard-to-reach fasteners.

Protect the torque converter during transmission removal. The converter can fall out and cause severe damage to both the converter and your feet. You can use a piece of band iron or even a box-end wrench with a bolt through the bellhousing to keep the converter in place.

linkages, 164-tooth flexplate, slip yoke, and hardware. This kit makes it easy to perform an AOD swap.

However, not everyone does a Mustang/Cougar AOD swap. There are plenty of swaps performed in other Ford vehicles such as the Maverick, Comet, Fairlane, Torino, F-Series trucks, Bronco, and a host of other vintage Fords. Conversion kits are available for many of them, but not all.

Ford Automatic Transmission Dimensions

All measurements are in inches. Information courtesy TCI Automotive.

C4 Case Fill (dipstick tube in the case)	
Overall Length	$24\frac{5}{16}$
Bell Face to Extension	$19\frac{1}{2}$
Bell Face to Mount	$16\frac{3}{4}$
Mount Width	$5\frac{9}{16}$
C4 Pan Fill (dipstick tube into the pan)	
Overall Length	$30\frac{19}{32}$
Bell Face to Extension	$20\frac{1}{2}$
Bell Face to Mount	$18\frac{1}{8}$
Mount Width	$5\frac{9}{16}$
C6 All Applications	
Overall Length	$33\frac{1}{2}$
Bell Face to Extension	$22\frac{3}{8}$
Bell Face to Mount	20
Mount Width	$5\frac{1}{2}$
AOD	
Overall Length	$30\frac{3}{8}$
Bell Face to Extension	$22\frac{5}{16}$
Bell Face to Mount	$20\frac{3}{16}$
Mount Width	$5\frac{5}{16}$
AODE/4R70W	
Overall Length	$31\frac{3}{16}$
Bell Face to Extension	$23\frac{5}{16}$
Bell Face to Mount	21
Mount Width	$5\frac{5}{16}$

California Pony Cars takes the guesswork out of an AOD swap. They have everything you need including crossmember, mount, 164-tooth flexplate, TV cable, manual linkage, and slip yoke.

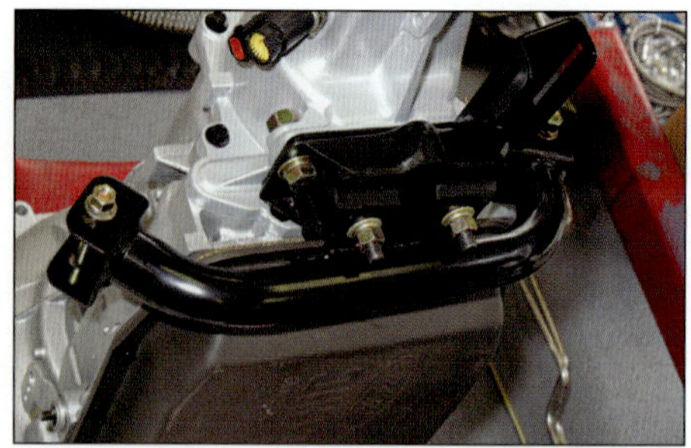

This is the California Pony Cars crossmember bolted to an AOD. It clears virtually everything including aftermarket headers. This is one of the better AOD crossmembers on the market.

If you're building a Ford, Mercury, or Lincoln and conversion kits are not available, you must have a crossmember and driveshaft made, which can get expensive. If you are so inclined, you can fabricate your own crossmember, but driveshaft fabrication must be performed by a qualified professional.

When you are swapping an AOD, it is important to recognize the differences between a C4 or early manual transmission and the AOD. The AOD takes a 164-tooth AOD-specific flexplate instead of the smaller 157-tooth pieces common to the C4 and early Ford manual transmissions. Because the AOD is longer, the crossmember must position the mount farther to the rear of the vehicle to support the transmission. There are no transmission-to-floorpan clearance issues with the AOD or AODE/4R70W in most applications except the Pinto, Bobcat, Mustang II, and Capri (prior to 1979).

Flexplate and Separator Plate Installation

This is the 157-tooth flexplate for the C4 transmission with a 28-ounce offset balance. You replace it with the 164-tooth flexplate for the AOD/AODE/4R70W, which is also a 28-ounce offset balanced. Note the type of engine you have also determines the flexplate type. Small-block Ford V-8s, which are externally balanced, are either 28- or 50-ounce offset balanced. Late-model 5.0L engines from 1982-up are 50-ounce. Earlier 289- and 302-ci small-blocks prior to 1982 are 28-ounce.

Here are two small-block Ford flexplates. On the left is the 157-tooth version for the C4 Cruise-O-Matic with a 28-ounce offset balance. On the right is the larger 164-tooth flexplate for AOD, AODE, and 4R70W with a 50-ounce offset balance. Small-block Fords prior to 1982 are normally 28-ounce offset balanced. Engines from 1982-up are 50-ounce offset balanced with a larger weight welded to the flexplate. This 164-tooth flexplate is 50-ounce offset balanced with a larger weight. If you're working with an unknown engine, you have to examine the flexplate to determine the offset balance.

1 Verify Torque Converter Fitment

Before installation, check torque converter dimensions. Also check the center hub diameter on a B&M torque converter. Although it doesn't happen very often, not all torque converters fit a Ford crank flange.

2 Check Crankshaft Flange Dimensions

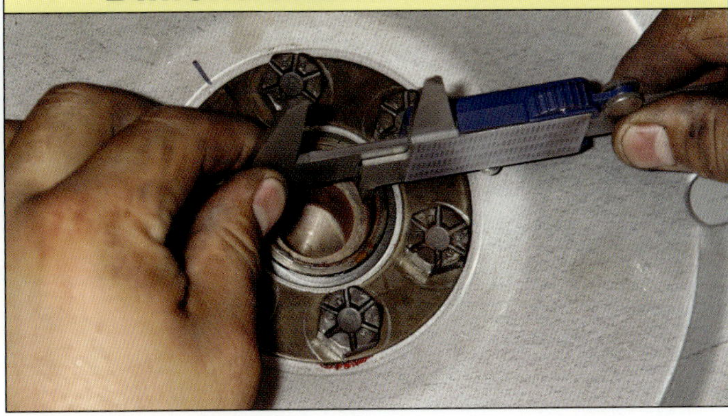

You must also check the crankshaft flange dimensions. Checking the converter hub and crank flange dimensions lets you know beforehand if the torque converter will fit during installation.

3 Install Flexplate

Use the reference mark you made during driveshaft removal to get the flexplate lined up perfectly for installation. There is only one way to install a flexplate because the bolt-hole pattern works only one way to prevent improper installation.

4 Choose Block Separator Plate

This universal block separator plate from Mike's Transmission goes between the engine block and bellhousing. It works with both 157- and 164-tooth flexplates as you can see by the perforated starter mount location (lower left).

5 Choose Block Separator Plate *CONTINUED*

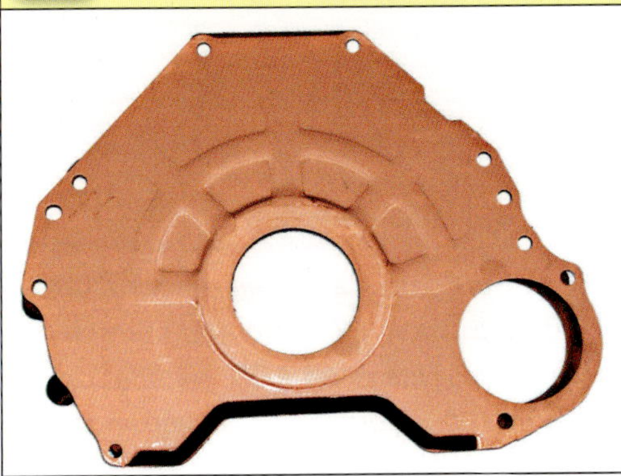

The AOD and C4 transmissions use different block plates primarily because they are different transmissions with two different-size flexplates. This means you need an AOD-specific block plate and dust cover for the 164-tooth flexplate.

Backup Light/Neutral Safety Switch Pin Locations

Pin Number	*Circuit Function*
1 & 2	Reverse Lights
3 & 4	Crank Only (Park and Neutral)

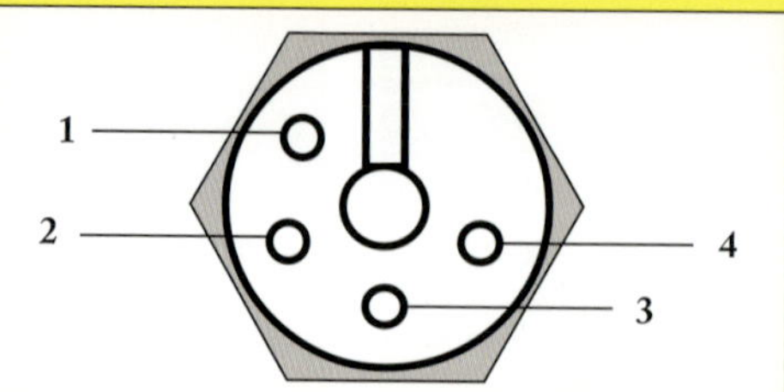

This simple wiring diagram (a top view of the neutral safety switch) shows pin identification for proper wiring into a vintage Ford wiring harness. Ford makes it easy to dovetail this plug into a vintage Ford wiring harness.

Because the AOD is longer, you need the appropriate-length driveshaft, which is available from a number of aftermarket suppliers. Mustangs Plus, for example, carries a complete line of ready-to-install Inland Empire Driveline driveshafts for these seemingly complicated swaps, which makes them uncomplicated.

Another important consideration with an AOD swap is the manual shift linkage and column shift versus floor shift. Aside from the obvious differences at the transmission with the manual shift lever pointing upward (column shift) or downward (console shift), you need to have a workable shifter on the driver's end. Floor-shift applications are easy to adapt using a 1967-up shifter, which has the proper detents. For column-shift

This is the AOD's multiplex plug for backup lights and neutral safety. If you cannot find a reproduction, it must come from a donor vehicle.

The backup light/neutral safety switch screws into the AOD case. As you move the manual shifter, you move a cam that moves this switch back and forth. In reverse, it grounds the backup light circuit. In any gear, there is an open ground in the start circuit, which prohibits starting. In park or neutral, the ground is complete and the engine starts.

Use proper installation equipment such as a transmission jack or a floor jack with a transmission cradle. Make sure the torque converter is properly seated. It is easy for the converter to slip off input shafts and pump drives and wind up with a faulty installation and pump failure. If you can fit your hand between the converter and the bellhousing, it is not properly seated.

Tom's Transmissions in Southern California demonstrates proper installation with the Lokar TV cable and manual linkage free and accessible. This is an AOD installation in an F-Series truck with 390 FE big-block power and a column shift.

applications, you will also need a 1967-up shifter, which can become complicated, depending upon model year and application. You should use 1967-up because of the shift detent positions. Ford Cruise-O-Matic applications prior to 1967 are not traditional P-R-N-D-2-1; instead, they have the Dual-Range Dot and Green Dot, where shift detents don't match the AOD shift pattern.

Console versus Column Shift

In your search for an AOD core, find out whether the core comes from a console or column shift. Column-shift applications call for the manual shift lever to be pointed downward. Console applications have the manual shift lever pointed upward.

There are also a variety of output shafts used in the AOD family of transmissions. Some have seven-tooth speedometer gears while others have eight-tooths. If you're going with an axle ratio greater than 3.27:1, you probably need the seven-tooth shaft. Those with 2.73:1 and 3.08:1 ratios have the eight-tooth shaft. ■

Lokar Manual Column-Shift Solutions

Lokar makes it easy to swap an AOD, AODE, or 4R70W into a vintage Ford. If you're going with a column shift, you need one of the following linkage kits.

- ACA-1807 for the AOD
- ACA-1808 for the AODE, 4R70W ■

This Lokar aftermarket column shift linkage on an F-Series truck tends to be more complex than a floor shift because there is more to it. Place the shifter in park and adjust the linkage from there. If you take your reference from park, everything else should fall into place.

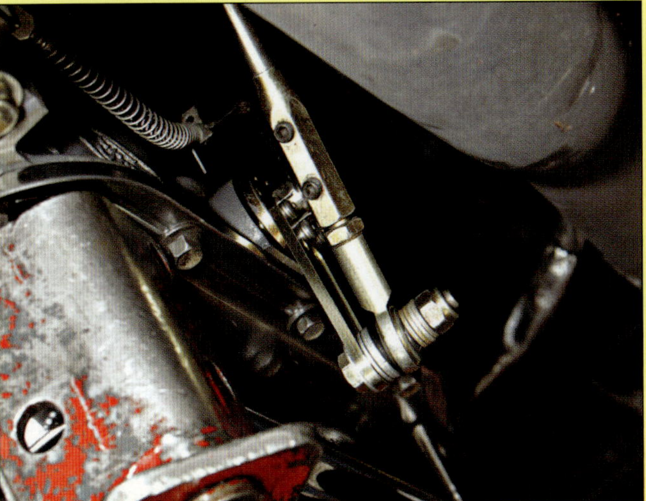

Here's the Lokar manual column shift linkage in proper adjustment. To the left is the TV cable for carburetion. The TV cable linkage is adjusted much the same way for factory and aftermarket linkages. More cable tension means a delayed upshift and greater line pressure. Less means a quicker upshift and slippage due to decreased line pressure.

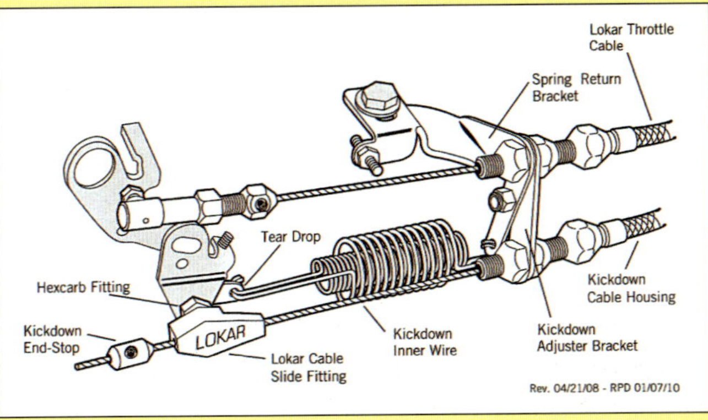

This is the Lokar AOD TV cable adjustment for carbureted vehicles. Cable tension can also be adjusted here. Cable adjustment is at the kickdown end stop. Loosen the Allen setscrew and either loosen or tighten the cable. You don't want tension, yet you don't want it too slack. (Illustration Courtesy Lokar Performance Products)

Try not to use rubber hose for your transmission cooler lines. If you must use hose, opt for braided stainless-steel hoses with commercial-grade clamps and keep hose length as short as possible. Make sure the hoses are not touching anything to prevent chaffing.

The AOD, AODE, and 4R70W transmissions are designed to accept a traditional mechanical cable-drive speedometer and an electronic version, depending upon your application.

Run transmission cooler lines parallel with the engine/transmission package all the way to the radiator or transmission cooler. This eliminates any chance of leakage and is much safer.

TECH TIP: Lokar Manual Shift Shaft Kits

Lokar offers a variety of manual shift shaft solutions for AOD, AODE, and 4R70W transmissions designed to work with nearly any application, including street rods.

Lokar PN	*Application*
ATA-1000	Ford AOD Selector Shaft and Arm 1/4" slot and hole
ATA-1001	Ford AOD Selector Shaft and Arm 5/16" slot
ATA-1002	Ford AODE/4R70W Selector Flange and Arm 1/4" slot and hole
ATA-1003	Ford AODE/4R70W Selector Flange and Arm 5/16" slot
ATA-1004	Ford AODE/4R70W Selector Flange and Arm 1/4" slot and hole
ATA-1005	Ford AODE/4R70W Selector Flange and Arm 5/16" slot ■

Up and Running

Begin transmission installation by adding 1 to 2 quarts of Dexron III or Mercon V transmission fluid to the torque converter to give both the converter and front pump a good fluid prime during initial firing. This fluid prime ensures plenty of lubrication on start-up plus immediate line pressure. Total fluid capacity is approximately 14 quarts. A huge percentage of this capacity is the torque converter once the engine fires and the converter fills.

When you fill the transmission sump, be conservative about how much fluid is added. Because transmission fluid expands as it warms, you do not want to fill to the "Full" mark cold. Overfilling the sump causes fluid foaming and malfunction. Foaming creates air in the fluid, undermining hydraulics and lubrication. Add transmission fluid to the minimum mark on the dipstick while cold and start the engine.

When you fire up the engine, listen for any abnormal noise and be prepared to immediately shut it down if you hear something. Any

TECH TIP: Bellhousing Difference

AOD, AODE, and 4R70W bellhousings come in two basic types: the 3.8L V-6 and 5.0L V-8 with a two-bolt starter bellhousing and the 4.6L Modular engine with a three-bolt starter bellhousing. When you're shopping for cores, pay attention to the starter to identify its application. Two-bolt starters are for overhead valve (OHV) small-block V-8 engines; three-bolt starters are for SOHC and DOHC V-8s. ■

squeal or metal-to-metal sound is an indication of improper torque converter installation or front pump/input shaft issues. If the torque converter has been improperly installed, it isn't engaging the pump and shafts properly. If this is the case, you have to remove the transmission and inspect for damage.

If there is damage and resulting metal particles are present in the fluid, the transmission must be torn down, inspected, and thoroughly cleaned. The torque converter must be replaced because it is virtually impossible to flush out contaminants.

If start-up is uneventful you are good to continue. With the engine at idle and the vehicle on a level surface, run the selector through all gear ranges and back to park. Make sure the parking brake is set and the selector is in park.

Torque converters must be serviced with a minimum of 1 to 2 quarts of Dexron III or Mercon V fluid for a good pump prime and a well-lubricated start-up. When the converter is installed, it fills the pump cavity with fluid.

It cannot be emphasized enough how important the flexplate-to-torque-converter alignment is. If your torque converter has a drain plug, make sure it is indexed properly at the flexplate. Otherwise, it presses into the flexplate, causing distortion and damage.

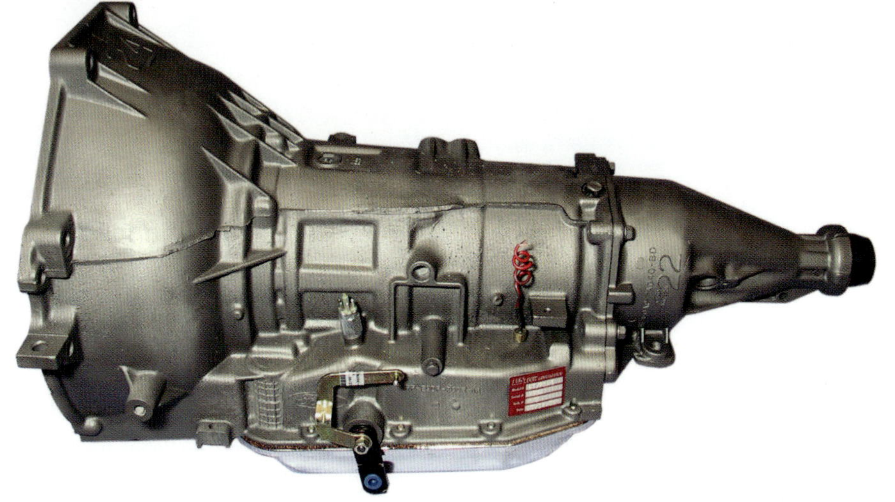
LenTech's reputation comes from making Ford's AOD, AODE, and 4R70W transmissions competitive in the marketplace and with enthusiasts. This is the LenTech Street Terminator AOD, which is rated to 800 hp with the one-piece billet input shaft, 1-2-3/4 shift pattern, improved line pressure for durability, heavy-duty clutches and bands, additional clutches, improved pump, and revised shift programming.

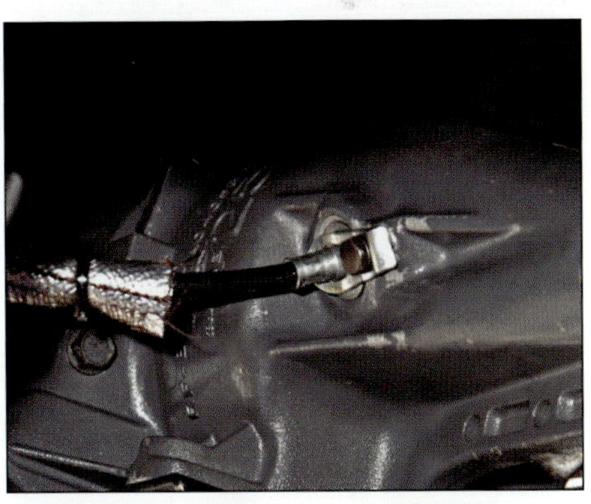
The AOD, AODE, and 4R70W are designed for either mechanical or electronic speedometer use. This is the mechanical cable-drive type. Speedometer gear selection depends on wheel and tire diameter (overall height). The more teeth the driven gear has, the lower the speedometer reads.

You can shorten your existing driveshaft for an AOD swap or have a shaft made. The California Pony Cars AOD conversion kit comes with a slip yoke, but not the shaft. You have a choice of steel or aluminum. Aluminum weighs less but isn't always the best choice for high-horsepower, high-torque applications.

When installing a new or modified driveshaft, harmonics (balance) can be an issue. Always have a driveshaft dynamic balanced. If you have vibration with a new driveshaft, rotating the shaft 180 degrees may eliminate it. If the vibration still exists, take the vehicle to a driveline specialist who can examine it for vibration issues.

AOD conversion kits aren't always available for all Ford applications. Some AOD swaps involve custom crossmember fabrication. Fabrication shops and hot rod shops are good sources for custom AOD and AODE/4R70W crossmembers. If you can provide the dimensions, most shops can fabricate the crossmember you need.

Ford used a torque converter dust cover for a reason: to keep both dust and foreign objects out of the bellhousing. If you don't have a dust shield, get one.

When you add fluid for the first time, bring it up to just below normal range on the dipstick. Remember, as the transmission warms, the fluid expands. If you top off at the "Full" mark cold, you will have fluid all over the garage floor when the sump reaches operating temperature. Add fluid in small amounts and allow the transmission to reach operating temperature. Run the selector through all ranges and re-check the fluid level. You want fluid at the 3/4 to "Full" mark hot. Never add fluid above the "Full" mark because it will cause foaming and erratic operation.

You can bolt the AOD/ AODE/4R70W to Ford's FE and 385-series big-blocks via conversion kits such as this Bendtsen's Speed Gems transmission adaptor.

"Line pressure" is just another way to describe hydraulic pressure. Screw this pressure gauge into the throttle valve pressure port on the passenger side and you get throttle valve pressure.

Adaptor kits use a crank spacer to move the flexplate aft into alignment with the bellhousing and torque converter. Adaptor kits are easy to use. It can get tricky at the transmission crossmember and mount, because not all kits have a crossmember. One may have to be fabricated.

Check the fluid again as the sump warms. When the transmission has reached operating temperature check the fluid level, which should be close to the "Full" mark. If it is overfull, you must siphon out excess fluid or face foaming and damage. Examine the dipstick at a hot idle and look for evidence of foaming (air bubbles) and any debris. Once the fluid level is stable and clear, you're ready for adjustment and a road test.

If you've installed an AODE or 4R70W it's a plug-and-play event with a road test and fluid check following start-up. Those first miles with the AODE and 4R70W are mostly a matter of getting to know the process for the PCM; it takes a while to map out a program before everything settles in. Shifts are unpredictable at first but then settle into a predictable routine. Expect to experience some slippage or even a harsh shift or two at first.

TV Cable Function

Before you embark upon TV cable adjustment, make sure the throttle cable or linkage is in proper adjustment and the throttle is wide open when the accelerator pedal is on the floor. With the accelerator pedal at rest, the throttle should be at idle stop. An AOD TV cable adjustment is pointless if everything else is out of adjustment.

The AOD calls for TV cable adjustment before taking the vehicle for a road test. It also calls for a pressure gauge at the throttle valve pressure port on the passenger side of the transmission case.

You need a pressure gauge (0 to 100 psi) screwed into the throttle valve pressure port on the passenger side of the transmission case. You also need a 1/8-inch NPT fitting to screw into the throttle valve port along with a minimum of 8 feet of heavy-duty hose that can withstand at least 100 psi so you can read the gauge from the driver's seat or engine compartment. Make sure the pressure gauge hose is well away from hot exhaust pipes. The throttle valve pressure port gives you throttled line pressure, which corresponds with throttle position.

At idle (throttle closed), you have low line pressure, which is what you want during deceleration and light throttle. With low line pressure, there is no cable tension (throttle closed) and virtually no shift felt (slippage). When the throttle is opened, cable movement and tension increase, modulating line pressure accordingly via the throttle valve, which is what you want when power is applied. The throttle valve does the work of both the vacuum modulator and kickdown on the C4, C6, and FMX. Rather than the intake manifold

This is the AOD's stock throttle valve and manual shift linkages. If you have a choice, this is the best setup to use because Ford has done all of the engineering work for you.

vacuum affecting line pressure, the throttle valve does it instead.

Adjusting the TV cable doesn't have to be a mystery, because thousands of new Fords rolled off the assembly line without a tedious TV cable adjustment. Assembly workers simply snapped a TV cable block pin into the closed throttle and locked the block and cable. You want a balance between cable tension and no cable tension with the cable slack, yet just short of tension. If you have a factory fuel-injected application, install the cable block at the closed throttle and lock the block with everything touching yet without cable tension. You want cable tension just as the throttle is coming off idle.

The same can be said for aftermarket cable packages such as Lokar's. The cable should be slack, with the throttle closed and the accelerator linkage relaxed. The cable must be snug, yet not tight. Lokar provides the necessary tools and information to properly adjust the TV cable.

Throttle Rod Adjustment

The throttle valve control rod connects the transmission's throttle valve lever and the carburetor/throttle body. When this throttle rod is properly adjusted, all you have to do is make minor adjustments at the throttle body or carburetor. The sliding trunnion block at the transmission normally doesn't require adjustment unless it has been apart. If both adjustments are where they should be, the throttle valve lever just inside the transmission is just touching the throttle valve without any pressure. In other words, the rod is limp with no pressure or tension. Accelerator pedal pressure, no matter how slight, moves the throttle valve.

With the engine at idle speed, set the parking brake firmly and place the shifter in neutral. Back the throttle valve rod adjustment (at the carburetor or throttle body) all the way out. Once the screw is flush with the lever's face, slowly turn it clockwise until the adjusting screw is just .005 inch from the throttle lever. Then turn the adjustment screw three additional turns clockwise. If it is not possible to turn the adjustment screw at least three full turns, the adjustment at the transmission is off and must be adjusted.

If you have to adjust the rod-style linkage at the transmission, loosen the bolt on the sliding trunnion and make sure the carburetor/throttle body end is firm against the throttle lever. Next, move the throttle valve lever at the transmission against the internal stop inside the transmission (not against the throttle valve) and tighten the trunnion bolt.

When you perform throttle valve rod adjustment using a pressure gauge, the engine and transmission should be at operating temperature. With the engine at idle against the throttle stop, insert a thickness gauge or drill bit (.394 inch, 10 mm, or 25/64 inch) between the throttle lever and throttle valve rod adjustment screw. Throttle valve pressure should be 30 to 40 psi. Turn the adjustment screw to achieve the ideal pressure of 33 psi. When the shifter is moved into gear, throttle valve pressure should rise 2 to 35 psi. Never adjust throttle valve pressure with the shifter in gear. Adjustments must be made in neutral.

When the gauge/drill bit is removed, the throttle valve pressure should drop to 5 psi. If the pressure is not 5 psi, back out the adjustment screw (counterclockwise) until the pressure drops to 5 psi. Then check the throttle valve pressure again with the thickness gauge or drill bit. It should be above 30 psi.

TV Cable Adjustment

There are two types of TV cable systems used on late-model Fords with port fuel injection. Although the two systems are different in function, they do essentially the same thing. Both pull a cable that operates the throttle valve. It's how far they pull the throttle cable that affects transmission shift function. With both types, you want the cable slack at idle, yet tension on the cable begins when the throttle comes off idle stop. This is what makes TV cable adjustment simple. You adjust the cable to where it has no tension at idle stop, yet it isn't slack, either.

The only difference between the two cable systems is how they adjust and lock down. It boils down to how far you're going to pull the cable and move the throttle valve to modulate line pressure. With some earlier AOD applications, you have a toggle-style adjustment at the throttle body. With the engine at idle, the parking brake set, the toggle adjuster unlocked, the transmission selector in neutral, and the T86L-70332-A gauge tool between the crimped slug on the cable end and the plastic fitting, push the cable slider forward slowly until pressure hits 33 psi.

Although Ford recommends using the special T86L-70332-A tool (available from a variety of aftermarket sources) to set the throttle valve pressure, you really don't need it. With the throttle at idle stop and the throttle valve lever inside the transmission just touching the throttle valve, you should see 5 psi.

The T86L-70332-A gauge tool is 10 mm in thickness, which means the cable end and adjuster should be 10 mm (25/64 inch) apart. You can make this tool yourself using flat washers stacked to this thickness and achieve the correct spacing, which should yield 33-psi pressure.

Then test-drive and pay close attention to shift quality and timing. If you get firm, well-timed upshifts and overdrive/lockup is in by 40 to 45 mph, the adjustment is good. Soft and sloppy early shifts mean poor adjustment. Once you get firm, well-timed upshifts, the goal is to get even better by making finite cable adjustments with more tension. If shifts become hard and delayed you've taken adjustment too far.

Late-model 5.0L High Output sequential electronic fuel injection Mustangs and the like have a notched self-locking rail adjuster, which is the easiest type of AOD throttle valve adjustment. On the notched rail, you have MIN (minimum), MID (midway), and MAX (maximum) cable travel. The key is to adjust enough cable tension into the system so line pressure corresponds with throttle position.

To adjust the self-locking rail adjuster, push in on the lock, which releases the notched rail and allows you to move the notched rail back and forth to adjust cable tension. With the cable completely slack, you should have 5-psi throttle valve pressure. Fit the T86L-70332-A gauge or your homemade spacer between the cable end and the adjuster in a snug fit. With the adjuster hooked to the throttle linkage and the engine at idle, you should see 33 psi.

These numbers are factory specifications. If you desire an even firmer shift, adjust the cable tighter in one-notch increments. You are safer going tighter than you are looser. Less cable tension and travel means low control pressure, slippage, and failure.

If you don't have a pressure gauge, you can still adjust AOD throttle valve pressure based on shift timing and firmness, although it is discouraged because everyone has a different perception of shift quality. The TV cable can be adjusted without a pressure gauge by very gently checking shift timing and quality with a road test. Begin TV cable adjustment as already suggested by having the TV cable straight and level yet without tension.

Road testing should deliver well-timed shift-points that are firm yet not harsh, yet all of the shifts (including overdrive) are in by 40 mph during light throttle. Soft shifts are a strong indication of slippage, which means you are burning clutches and bands. Remember, you can burn up an AOD in short order with improper TV cable adjustment and a WOT.

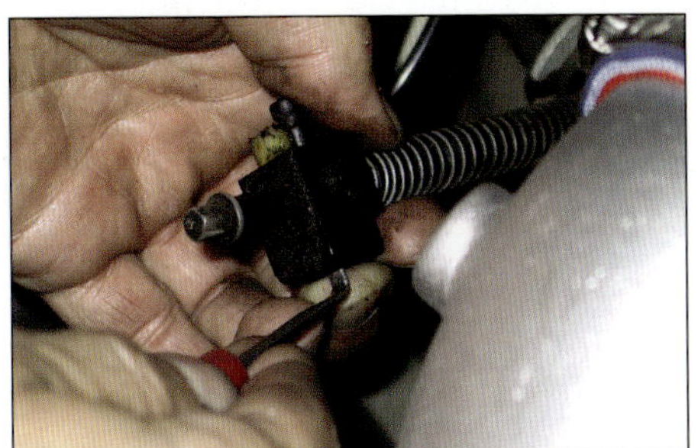

This is the AOD's factory TV cable adjustment with sequential electronic fuel injection (SEFI). It is a notched plastic unit requiring finite tuning one notch at a time that adjusts cable tension. The more tension you have, the later and harder the shift. When you have more cable tension, you get higher line pressure and a delayed upshift. Ideally, you have a nice balance of line pressure and shift timing.

The equivalent of the T86L-70332-A TV cable adjustment gauge fits between the cable adjuster and cable end (arrow). With the cable pulled 25/64 inch (10 mm) and locked at this dimension, you should have 33-psi throttle valve pressure at idle in neutral. Set the adjustment, remove the gauge, and you should have 5 psi. You can make this gauge with a stack of washers glued together to a thickness of 25/64 inch (10 mm).

TECH TIP

Lokar Part Numbers

If you're swapping an AOD into a carbureted Ford, look to Lokar's cable (PN KD2AODHT) and bracket (PN SRK4000). Both make it easy to put an AOD behind your carbureted engine, and adjustment is easy. ■

Source Guide

B&M Racing & Performance
9142 Independence Ave.
Chatsworth, CA 91311
818-882-6422
bmracing.com

Leon's Transmission
7528 Reseda Blvd.
Reseda, CA 91335
818-345-8101
leonstransmission.com

Mike's Transmission
42541 6th St. E., #11
Lancaster, CA 93535
661-723-0081
mikestransmission.com

Performance Automatic
8174 Beechcraft Ave.
Gaithersburg, MD 28079
301-963-8078
performanceautomatic.com

TCI Automotive
151 Industrial Dr.
Ashland, MS 38603
888-776-9824
tciauto.com

Tom's Transmissions
16609 Sierra Hwy.
Canyon Country, CA 91351
661-251-3438
tomstrans.com

Transmission Rebuilding Company
10140 Topanga Canyon Blvd.
Chatsworth, CA 91311
800-987-2676
trctransmission.com

Transmission Parts & Cores
1981 W. Winton Ave.
Hayward, CA 94545
510-783-5222
transmissionpartsandcores.com

Transtar Industries, Inc.
7350 Young Dr.
Cleveland, OH 44146
800-359-3339
transtar1.com

TransGo
2621 Merced Ave.
El Monte, CA 91733
626-443-7451
transgo.com